The Complete Guide to

TRUST AND ESTATE MANAGEMENT:

What You Need to Know About Being a Trustee or an Executor Explained Simply

By Gerald Shaw

With Foreword By Linda C. Ashar, Attorney at Law

THE COMPLETE GUIDE TO TRUST AND ESTATE MANAGEMENT: WHAT YOU NEED TO KNOW ABOUT BEING A TRUSTEE OR AN EXECUTOR EXPLAINED SIMPLY

Copyright © 2011 Atlantic Publishing Group, Inc.
1405 SW 6th Avenue • Ocala, Florida 34471 • Phone 800-814-1132 • Fax 352-622-1875
Web site: www.atlantic-pub.com • E-mail: sales@atlantic-pub.com
SAN Number: 268-1250

Library of Congress Cataloging-in-Publication Data

Shaw, Gerald, 1953-
  The complete guide to trust and estate management : what you need to know about being a trustee or an executor explained simply / by Gerald Shaw.
     p. cm.
  Includes bibliographical references and index.
  ISBN-13: 978-1-60138-201-6 (alk. paper)
  ISBN-10: 1-60138-201-4 (alk. paper)
  1. Trusts and trustees--United States--Popular works. 2. Trusts and trustees--Taxation--United States--Popular works. 3. Executors and administrators--United States--Popular works. 4. Inheritance and transfer tax--Law and legislation--United States--Popular works. I. Title.
  KF730.Z9S49 2010
  346.7305'6--dc22
                              2008032591

PROJECT MANAGER: Melissa Peterson • mpeterson@atlantic-pub.com
PEER REVIEWER: Marilee Griffin • EDITOR: Cindy House
EDITORIAL ASSISTANT: Amy Gronauer • INTERIOR DESIGN: Samantha Martin
PRE-PRESS & PRODUCTION DESIGN: Holly Marie Gibbs
BACK COVER DESIGN: Jackie Miller • millerjackiej@gmail.com

Printed on Recycled Paper

We recently lost our beloved pet "Bear," who was not only our best and dearest friend but also the "Vice President of Sunshine" here at Atlantic Publishing. He did not receive a salary but worked tirelessly 24 hours a day to please his parents. Bear was a rescue dog that turned around and showered myself, my wife, Sherri, his grandparents Jean, Bob, and Nancy, and every person and animal he met (maybe not rabbits) with friendship and love. He made a lot of people smile every day.

We wanted you to know that a portion of the profits of this book will be donated to The Humane Society of the United States. *–Douglas & Sherri Brown*

The human-animal bond is as old as human history. We cherish our animal companions for their unconditional affection and acceptance. We feel a thrill when we glimpse wild creatures in their natural habitat or in our own backyard.

Unfortunately, the human-animal bond has at times been weakened. Humans have exploited some animal species to the point of extinction.

The Humane Society of the United States makes a difference in the lives of animals here at home and worldwide. The HSUS is dedicated to creating a world where our relationship with animals is guided by compassion. We seek a truly humane society in which animals are respected for their intrinsic value, and where the human-animal bond is strong.

Want to help animals? We have plenty of suggestions. Adopt a pet from a local shelter, join The Humane Society and be a part of our work to help companion animals and wildlife. You will be funding our educational, legislative, investigative and outreach projects in the U.S. and across the globe.

Or perhaps you'd like to make a memorial donation in honor of a pet, friend or relative? You can through our Kindred Spirits program. And if you'd like to contribute in a more structured way, our Planned Giving Office has suggestions about estate planning, annuities, and even gifts of stock that avoid capital gains taxes.

Maybe you have land that you would like to preserve as a lasting habitat for wildlife. Our Wildlife Land Trust can help you. Perhaps the land you want to share is a backyard— that's enough. Our Urban Wildlife Sanctuary Program will show you how to create a habitat for your wild neighbors.

So you see, it's easy to help animals. And The HSUS is here to help.

THE HUMANE SOCIETY
OF THE UNITED STATES

2100 L Street NW • Washington, DC 20037 • 202-452-1100
www.hsus.org

TRADEMARK STATEMENT

All trademarks, trade names, or logos mentioned or used are the property of their respective owners and are used only to directly describe the products being provided. Every effort has been made to properly capitalize, punctuate, identify and attribute trademarks and trade names to their respective owners, including the use of ® and ™ wherever possible and practical. Atlantic Publishing Group, Inc. is not a partner, affiliate, or licensee with the holders of said trademarks.

DEDICATION

This book is dedicated to my aunt, Jean Cusick,
for being there when I needed her.

TABLE OF CONTENTS

Chapter 7: Preparations After Death 107

Chapter 8: Probate 115

Chapter 9: Administering the Estate 127

Chapter 10: Tax Considerations 135

FOREWORD

The business of death is never easy and certainly not simple in our modern world. All manner of details require attention, even when the deceased leaves few assets behind. Many of these details are required by law and involve a maze of court and other bureaucratic procedures, which vary from state to state.

The personal representative has a fiduciary duty to ensure all the responsibilities entrusted to his or her care are properly and timely executed. When involved in the probate court, the personal representative also becomes an officer of the court. This important duty is further compounded by the stress that death inevitably brings, for the personal representative is nearly always someone who was close to the deceased. Handling an estate can span a variety of experiences for the personal representative, from the routine to the slightly bizarre.

A recent example is the estate of Clifford Lassmann in Waukesha County, Wisconsin. Lassmann died on August 18, 2007, at age 67, when he was trampled by a horse boarded at his Sundrift Stables. In his will, he bequeathed all to his best friend Jackie Vogel, who was also named as the estate's personal representative.

Lassmann did not leave anything to his two adult daughters, although one daughter would inherit if Vogel failed to survive him by 30 days. This daughter sued the estate and Vogel, contesting ownership of Lassmann's Morgan gelding, Sundrift City Slicker aka "Iggy." The daughter claimed ownership of Iggy. Vogel produced an updated transfer agreement purporting to show that the daughter signed Iggy over to her father before Lassmann died. The change in ownership was never registered with the American Morgan Horse Association Registry.

Vogel was seeking to sell Iggy on behalf of the estate. Lassmann's daughter wanted the horse. The argument went into court mediation. During these proceedings, Iggy died. The court eventually decided in favor of the daughter, awarding Iggy's ashes, his tail, and $50,000 in proceeds from other assets of the estate to Lassmann's daughter.

As the Lassmann estate shows, the personal representative may have to juggle personal interests with formal fiduciary duties. Protecting the estate's interests may require court proceedings, appraisals, and verification of documents. Thus, the personal representative's job is a multi-dimensional process, often requiring a balancing of complex legal and family interests with those of the deceased, especially where a will or trust is involved.

It is because there are such competing interests, especially within families, that a personal representative is required by law to represent the estate — that is, the interest of the deceased. In a very real sense, it is the final act the personal representative performs for a friend or loved one.

Such matters as arranging for burial or cremation, ensuring the deceased's affairs are properly handled according to his or her wishes (if possible), fielding creditors, finding beneficiaries, getting appraisals, finding and counting assets, keeping records, sorting personal property, filing tax returns, satisfying legal requirements as they relate to next of kin and the government, and a myriad of other tasks are the responsibility of the person who is appointed as the personal representative of the deceased person's estate. This may be someone who is named by the deceased in his or her will as executor or appointed by the court as administrator of the estate. In some cases, there may be so few assets that a formal court process is not required, but the deceased's affairs will still require final resolution by a personal representative.

Understanding the scope of the personal representative's duties is only the first step. Stop there and the task will only loom large and daunting. It need not. *The Complete Guide to Trust and Estate Management* provides a complete guideline to demystify this important job, providing not just the what, but the how and why to navigate the process of managing the business of an estate easily and wisely.

—Linda C. Ashar, Attorney at Law

About Linda C. Ashar

Linda C. Ashar is a lawyer, educator, horse breeder, freelance writer, and artist. Her law practice encompasses more than 29 years before the Ohio and Federal Bars. She is a senior shareholder in the firm of Wickens, Herzer, Panza, Cook & Batista Co. in Avon, Ohio. In addition to her juris doctor in law, she has a master's of art in special education and bachelor's of art in English.

She is professional writer and has authored *101 Ways to Score Higher on Your LSAT: What You Need to Know About the Law School Admission Test Explained Simply* (Atlantic Publishing Group, Inc. 2008), poetry, and several magazine and journal articles.

She is an Adjunct Professor at DeVry University and a frequent speaker at law seminars.

She and her lawyer-husband, Mike, operate Thornapple Farms in Vermilion, Ohio, where they breed Morgan Horses, including rare Lippitt Morgan bloodstock, Connemara Ponies, and Irish Kerry Bog Ponies, a critically endangered breed. Ashar serves on several nonprofit boards and is co-founder of Elysian Fields: The Justin Morgan Association for Retired Equines and the American Kerry Bog Pony Society.

Her interpretive art has been showcased by Mac Worthington Gallery in Columbus, Ohio; she paints by private commission, with subjects including equines, portraits, and landscapes. You can reach her at ashar@hbr.net or lashar@wickenslaw.com.

INTRODUCTION

Before I became the personal representative for an estate (also referred to as *executor* or *administrator*, depending on the legal procedure involved), I had no idea what the job of handling an estate entailed. My mother was well prepared for her death. She had consulted with an attorney and knew that in her state — Florida — the estate is automatically divided among the children equally. She had two children who pretty much knew what to expect. Therefore, she had little to plan. Her finances were all in order. Her property was paid for and would be transferred easily when the time came. There were no conflicts within the family. My brother and I were expecting the inevitable.

Although dealing with the death of a loved one is deeply saddening, it was heartening to have something to remember our mother by and to know we were fortunate to inherit what we did. We went through the normal bereavement process, which just about everyone must face at some time in life. Still, despite the grieving period and emotions involved, we eventually needed to distribute the property and assets formally. It was not a problem, I thought. It was, frankly, the last thing on my mind. Dealing with my mother's death was the center of everything. Changing the names on the property title would be something routine.

I remember calling the county clerk's office and explaining the situation: *My mother has passed away, and we have to change the name on papers so that tax statements can go to the right person. State law says my brother and I each get half of the estate, and there is no conflict. So, just send over the paperwork, and we will sign it.* I was naïve enough to believe I could do everything over the phone in a few minutes and have it verified in a few days.

Then I heard the person on the other end of the line mention "probate," a word that sounded familiar, yet foreign. The property would have to go through the probate court, she explained. I would need to see an attorney who specializes in probate. It was not something I could do myself, she told me. (Well, I could, but any amateurish mistake could tie up the property for years until the legal matters were straightened out properly. Just one more thing I had to worry about.)

Though I would learn that probate is a relatively simple process to understand, I was fortunate to have extended family to turn to for help. My aunt's attorney put me in touch with a lawyer who specialized in estate matters and who explained the details clearly, making the entire process as painless as possible.

Probate is a legal procedure through which the deceased person's assets are passed to his or her beneficiaries under court supervision according to state law. The court's role is to ensure that the assets are administered properly, that all beneficiaries receive a share of the estate, and that all creditors of the estate are paid.

If the deceased person had a will, the court ensures that the terms and conditions of his or her wishes are carried out. If there is no will, the court follows state law governing distribution of intestate estates. I was once again fortunate that my mother's estate was handled easily, compared with the complexities of other estates that involve many more assets and an extended number of heirs or business interests.

My brother agreed to my appointment as personal representative for the estate. Occasionally, following consultations in the office or over the phone, my attorney would send me papers to sign and return, and he filed the papers with the court. He provided insight during each stage of the process, explaining in easy-to-understand terms what was going on and why it was necessary. In a few months, probate was completed, and the property title was transferred to my brother and me.

Again, handling my mother's estate was relatively simple. No one estate is the same as another. Each personal representative has specific duties and responsibilities. The representative may have only one property to deal with, or several different types to disburse to a variety of beneficiaries. The collection and payment of debts, calculating taxes, filing forms, inventorying and appraising assets, handling the deceased person's final affairs, and arranging details of all other estate matters will be different for every personal representative.

The same is true for the trustee, who handles a property similar to the probate estate. The difference is that the property is confined within the terms of a trust. The trustee must follow the trust agreement, which is a governing document made by the trust's creator (also called the grantor or trustor). The grantor sets up guidelines for holding, managing, and investing the trust assets and directs who receives income and assets from the trust (the trust beneficiaries) and how income from the trust is paid out. The trustee holds the legal title to the trust property until the trust's terms are completed.

This book will discuss in detail the responsibilities of the personal representative and the trustee, as well as issues that may arise as they perform their duties.

The personal representative of an estate is entrusted with the management of property and will always be acting on behalf of the estate. You must know how to deal with grief-stricken and sometimes angry beneficiaries, as well as understand fully the time and effort involved before taking on this important job. Your role may be as simple as handling the deceased person's wishes or as complex as settling quarrels among relatives involved in business transactions. You will organize assets, pay debts, manage an entire estate, and interact with professionals until the process is completed.

You must also be concerned with legal matters, such as avoiding liability. What happens if you sell an asset without authority and beneficiaries lose interest on the income? Or, you could spend estate money, which the court could later consider as a negligent action. What happens if there is a conflict of interest, or if you make financial decisions without proper counsel? You are also liable for the actions of co-personal representatives who may be assigned to handle different areas of the estate.

For example, you should document all investment decisions. Showing the court that you kept accurate financial records and periodically reviewed your decisions helps avoid potential lawsuits. Communicating with beneficiaries is important and will help form a solid relationship that will naturally deter any conflict. Discussion of estate transactions will promote compromise and agreement among all parties.

You should keep receipts for any assets that you distribute. Beneficiaries should provide written consent to you whenever investments are changed. A smart personal representative may obtain a release or consent form waiving liability as long as the beneficiary is aware of all relevant facts. A court order for a particular action can protect you from future liability. You should always be timely in filing necessary information, but you should also take the time to be careful when distributing assets. Some beneficiaries might be eager to collect money they believe is owed to them, but the probate and administrative process can be time-consuming. Your duty is to make proper and organized decisions in a timely and responsible manner.

A trustee has similar, but also different, responsibilities. Your duties include assembling, protecting, and investing the trust's assets. You must adhere to standards of conduct to carry out the duties given to you through the trust agreement. You need to exercise care and diligence in managing the trust. These obligations are referred to as fiduciary responsibilities. As with personal representatives for probate estates, trustees should perform tasks in a timely and effective manner. You should call on legal and financial professionals for guidance whenever necessary. You can make discretionary distributions in accordance with the trust grantor's intent. You also will recognize the beneficiary's needs and use reasonable judgment in carrying out the distributions. You need to keep accurate records of each distribution and should maintain those records for the life of the trust.

Personal representatives and trustees must become acquainted with paying debts, expenses, and taxes. Tax laws vary from state to state. As representatives of an estate or trust, you must familiarize yourself with the deadlines for filing tax returns. If you are a trustee, you will need to pay any outstanding fees, commissions, and expenses incurred during your administration of the trust. Sometimes, you will need to use the trust's assets solely to satisfy obligations of the estate.

From the beginning, the difficult task of minimizing estate taxes will be a concern. For example, deductions and credits are allowed for funeral expenses, debts, administrative costs, legal and accounting fees, and casualty or theft losses. You can also deduct charitable contributions and certain claims against the estate. You may be able to apply credits to estate taxes, if any, owed to the state.

Understanding the duties of a personal representative or trustee may seem difficult at first. However, the more you learn, the more you understand the reasons for such positions and how important it is to administer property and assets in the best interests of a deceased person's loved ones.

CHAPTER 1

The Role of Personal
Representative/Trustee

Being a personal representative or trustee is an honor and a great responsibility. The job can require a significant amount of time and commitment, depending on the estate. As handler of the estate, you must abide by certain legal, ethical, and moral standards because you are not only acting in accordance with the deceased person's wishes, but also in the beneficiary's best interest.

Handling the Estate

As a personal representative, you must understand the job's basic responsibilities and know whom to contact when you need assistance. The person assigned to control an estate could be appointed by the deceased person before his or her death, or through court proceedings. A will or trust can also name the overseer of an estate. If no one is assigned to the task, the court will step in to appoint a personal representative according to state and local laws.

A personal representative's job can be easy and hard, fun and boring, and exciting and aggravating. If you are interested in taking charge of something that matters, this can be your chance to be a major influence in people's lives. Someone must be in charge of the property left by a person who dies.

Any person 18 years or older who has not been convicted of a felony can serve as a personal representative or trustee. The person serving in one of these roles can be a qualified lawyer, accountant, or financial consultant, or even someone close to the deceased person, such as a spouse, adult child, relative, or a friend.

Although being appointed as a personal representative is an honor, you must consider whether you have the ability, time, or desire to take on the role. You also have to consider location. Are you near the estate and the beneficiaries involved? You have the right to refuse or renounce the appointment if you think the responsibility will be too much for you to handle or think it would not be in the best interests of the beneficiaries or the deceased person's wishes.

Experience in financial matters and management can be beneficial in handling an estate. You may be running the deceased person's investment accounts or business. You will be responsible for making decisions about continuing or terminating the business. It could be a partnership, in which you might have to step in to do what you were instructed to do or act on your best judgment. You do not necessarily have to be knowledgeable in all matters of the estate, but you should know whom to go to for advice and how to deal with investments properly and soundly.

Some of the tasks you will be doing as a personal representative include:

- Taking care of the inventory, appraisals, and distribution of the deceased person's assets

- Paying taxes, which will involve estate and inheritance taxes, as well as filing a final income-tax return

- Paying bills for the estate, including funeral costs

- Collecting money owed to the estate

- Overseeing the investment of assets in the estate

- Settling the deceased person's debts and notifying creditors according to state law

- Following the deceased person's wishes and intentions, particularly when they are specified in a will

- Seeking the help and guidance of professionals, such as attorneys, financial advisers, or property and insurance agents

- Completing all settlements with the probate court

Personal representatives and trustees are entrusted with the management of the property, which can involve a variety of factors. The estate could be as simple as carrying out the deceased person's wishes, or as complex as settling quarrels and property disputes among heirs and outsiders. Because you may be acting on behalf of the beneficiaries, you could be dealing with family members going through a grieving process. Before taking on these responsibilities, you should know how to deal with family situations while simultaneously handling the estate.

Since you will be organizing the estate's assets and handling all financial matters, you must be very careful in your actions. You are liable if you sell assets without authority, spend estate money in a manner the court considers negligent, have conflicts of interest, or make final decisions without proper counsel. These actions may cause financial losses for the beneficiaries and bring about legal problems for you.

You need to document the investment decisions you make and periodically update the court on your actions. Frequent communication with beneficiaries is important because it builds a solid relationship that will help prevent future conflicts.

You should be timely when it comes to filing necessary information and distributing any assets. The probate process can be time-consuming, and those in line to collect might be eager to get their share. You will be following up on many details, defending the terms of the will if you have to, and performing the necessary duties to preserve the estate's value by paying expenses and taxes.

Handling an estate does not have to be difficult, especially if you know who to turn to when making professional decisions. You will work closely with an estate attorney who knows when and how to file the necessary legal documents with the court. The attorney also advises you on financial or property matters, or recommends a professional for advice. You can rely heavily on this guidance while taking responsibility for keeping the estate in good order, protecting any assets, and safely making the correct investments with the estate's funds. This also helps you avoid any liability with the beneficiaries.

Large estates may be very complicated and often require years in probate court. If you choose to excuse yourself from such a difficult task, the court will appoint an alternate personal representative or successor unless the will provides for an alternate person willing to serve. Co-personal representatives also can be designated to handle an estate. A court or a person writing a will may appoint a family member to handle one portion of the estate, and appoint a financial adviser or banking institution to take care of other affairs. Sometimes, many co-personal representatives handle the various aspects of a large estate. This can be done by court decision or through the deceased person's choice as expressed in the will.

ESTATE PLANNING TIPS

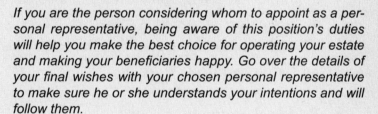

Anyone wishing to name someone as personal representative or trustee would be wise to first ask that person if he or she is willing to serve in this role.

If you are the person considering whom to appoint as a personal representative, being aware of this position's duties will help you make the best choice for operating your estate and making your beneficiaries happy. Go over the details of your final wishes with your chosen personal representative to make sure he or she understands your intentions and will follow them.

Here are a few important terms to remember in handling an estate or trust:

- **Fiduciary**: A person or trust company acting on behalf of another. Trustees and personal representatives are fiduciaries.

- **Grantor**: Also called settler, creator, or trustor, a person who operates property by means of a trust and/or whose wishes are expressed in the trust.

- **Testator**: Someone who has made a valid will. A woman is sometimes called a testatrix.

- **Beneficiary**: A person who is named in and benefits from the will or trust as a recipient of assets and/or income.

- **Trustee**: The person or trust company that holds legal title to the trust property for the benefit of another (beneficiary), acting in accordance with the terms of the trust.

- **Personal representative**: The person or trust company settling the estate according to the terms of a deceased person's will or as appointed by the probate court. When appointed by a will, the term for this position is usually executor; a woman is sometimes called an executrix. When appointed by a court, the term may be administrator/administratrix.

- **Principal**: Property or capital of an estate.

- **Income**: Returns from the property of an estate, including interest, dividends, or rent. Gains resulting from appreciation in value may also be income.

Standards and Decision-Making

A personal representative or trustee must stick to the documented instructions of the will or trust and should seek professional advice or clarification from the court when certain matters are not specified. Your wide range of duties may include making repairs or improvements to property, selling property, employing attorneys or accountants, paying taxes and insurance, settling claims, and handling investments and other functions according to state laws, estate codes, and court decisions. You must remain loyal, impartial, and dedicated to the estate/trust's directives while avoiding conflicts of interest that may overlap with your own financial holdings and concerns.

You must keep the interests of the beneficiaries in mind whenever taking an action regarding the estate. For example, risk-taking or speculating may be fine for you when dealing with investments or real estate for your personal portfolio. If you lose, it is your loss. As a trustee or personal representative, however, you are not acting for yourself. The interests of the beneficiaries, along with the deceased person's wishes and intentions, will be your guiding light. It is not necessarily your job to invest funds from the estate with the intention of maximizing those funds for the beneficiaries. Carefully consider any investment so you keep those funds secure and intact for the heirs.

Most people select a personal representative or trustee based on whom they feel they can trust to settle their affairs. The key word is trust. As a personal representative or trustee, you have a fiduciary relationship with the deceased person's final instructions, and this relationship is based on trust. The laws that govern estate and trust administration are designed to ensure this trust is not broken. A fundamental understanding of what these laws and standards of conduct mean can substantially reduce any risks involved in being the overseer of an estate.

The powers given to you in the administration of an estate, according to a will or trust agreement, may include retaining and receiving assets, selling or exchanging property, investing assets, taking control of real estate, employing professionals, borrowing funds, settling claims, negotiating claims, paying taxes and other expenses, continuing business and other ventures, and insuring assets.

Some wills or trusts might limit what you may do. For example, they may prohibit the sale of certain assets. All estates and estate plans are unique. It is extremely important for you to examine the will and any documents or instructions left by the deceased person.

Loyalty is a major duty and function when handling an estate. A trustee might administer the trust solely in the interest of the beneficiaries. A personal representative might administer the estate for the benefit of the creditors until the necessary payments are made, and then for the beneficiaries.

Loyalty to the estate means you should not put yourself in a position where self-interest will influence the performance of your duties. You may not profit at the expense of a beneficiary or creditor. If you have the power to sell property, you may not buy it or otherwise acquire any interest in the asset, even if you purchase it at a fair market price. This would be in conflict with your duties because you would not necessarily be selling the property at the highest price for the beneficiaries. You are allowed to receive only the legal fees for services you provide. As a reminder, here are some ways to avoid or limit your liability:

- Read the trust and estate documents.

- Seek clarification from an attorney or instructions from the court if the terms of a will or trust are misleading or ambiguous.

- Hire professionals to assist you with administration tasks you do not have time for, or that you lack the expertise to handle.

- Communicate with beneficiaries about the administration of the estate or trust on a regular basis.

- Keep accurate and current records.

- Take possession and protect all assets of the estate or trust.

- Review and monitor the activities of all professional agents that you hire.

- Do not mix estate or trust assets with your own.

- Do not purchase from, or sell assets to, an estate or trust if you are the personal representative or trustee.

- Do not employ yourself to perform special tasks for a special fee, such as appraisals, accounting services, or property management.

- Do not borrow money from the estate or trust.

- Do not accept gifts or commissions from someone who does business with the estate or trust.

- Do not share confidential information with individuals who do not have an interest in the estate or trust.

- Always act with the standards of conduct of a personal representative or trustee in mind.

You should always remain impartial when dealing with the parties involved in the estate. You may not favor one beneficiary over the other. You also must balance the competing interests of the current beneficiaries, who are concerned about the assets they have, and the future beneficiaries, who want those assets to grow.

Personal representatives and trustees should exercise the same skill and care they would use when dealing with their own property, if not more so, making sure all assets are protected and not lost or destroyed.

You must make sure the estate's assets and property are kept separate from your own property. You should keep up-to-date and accurate records of the activities of the estate or trust. Although professional help is necessary at times, you should not delegate the duties that you can reasonably perform. You are obligated to perform your duties in a reasonable manner and should not transfer any responsibilities to others unless authorized to do so under the terms of the will or trust documents.

Some other obligations of a personal representative or trustee include:

- Pay income to the beneficiaries, according to the terms of the will and the trust.

- Stand ready to defend third-party claims against the estate or trust, and also enforce claims held by the estate or trust.

- Keep the beneficiaries informed throughout your tenure as the estate's overseer. If you do not keep close contact with them, they could sue you if something goes wrong. No matter how well you do your job, you can make mistakes. Beneficiaries may be more forgiving if they have a close relationship with you and understand what is going on.

Remember, your fundamental duty as a personal representative is loyalty, which means you need to have a strong relationship with the beneficiaries. You are not turning your life over to them, but you must act in their benefit. This relationship should be confidential, so do not discuss it with unauthorized people or outsiders.

As a fiduciary charged with protecting the assets of the estate, you should use reasonable care and skill to make the property and investments productive, secure, and profitable, as long as you keep any decisions within the guidelines and directions of the will or trust. The court and the law will monitor your conduct only to make sure you are behaving reasonably. They will not automatically judge poor performance to be your fault. If you are found to have acted with imprudent, reckless, or intentionally bad conduct, you can be liable if losses result.

This is why maintaining an accurate record of actions and reasons for your decisions reduces your liability as overseer of the estate. Examples of being negligent and subject to liability include selling an asset without authority, resulting in a loss; engaging in obvious conflicts of interest; or spending money that results in a loss. You also may be responsible for the actions of co-personal representatives involved in other areas of the estate. You must act prudently at all times. Some estates are easier to handle than others, but it is still your responsibility no matter the size.

The Probate Process

Among your first duties as personal representative of an estate is initiating probate, the court's formal process of proving the authenticity of the deceased person's will, instructions, and assets. The court also will verify your assignment as estate representative. You might want to consult with a qualified probate or estate attorney first, as either you or the attorney will have to file an application with the probate court. You can get the filing information from your attorney or through the clerk of the probate court, which you can find in government listings or the local phone book. You also need to notify the beneficiaries that probate proceedings are under way. You can charge attorney's fees to the estate as an expense.

Either you or your attorney will appear in probate court with the original signed will and a certified copy of the death certificate.

Along with legal fees, the estate can cover court costs if needed. Either you or the attorney will handle these transactions. The probate court will decide the will's validity, which is usually a routine affair, although anyone may challenge or contest the will at this time. Anyone wishing to challenge a will or any part of it has to file an official objection with the court within a certain amount of time, as stipulated by state law. Challenges to a will can disrupt the probate process and can become time-consuming and costly to the estate and everyone involved.

The Probate Court Judge

Probate court is part of a state's court system; some states have special judges who only handle estate settlement cases, while others might not specialize in that way. Regardless of the laws governing the organizational structure of the court, a probate judge will review the legal documents related to an estate. If a person dies without a will, the judge will appoint an administrator, who serves in the same capacity as an executor. He or she will also ask for and review documents, such as the will (if there is one), the inventory of assets, and petitions from creditors and heirs. Heir is the legal title of a person who inherits property from an estate that does not have a will, or is intestate; beneficiaries are those who receive an inheritance by being named in a legal document like a will or trust.

The judge will supervise the process of settling your estate and will only adjudicate, or hand down decisions, as they are needed, such as when a creditor makes a claim and is denied payment by the administrator. The same can be done when a person comes forward and claims to be an heir to your estate.

Probate judges also establish guardianship and handle other special circumstances, such as bigamy, live-in lovers who want part of an estate, or "long-lost children" who contest decisions regarding heirs.

After the probate court declares the will valid, you will begin paying taxes and other claims against the estate. You also may begin distributing assets to the beneficiaries. However, if the will is found to be invalid, you must proceed as if it did not exist. In the meantime, the court will appoint a personal representative. Creditors and taxes must still be paid. The remainder of the estate will be distributed to the correct people and places according to state law.

Assuming the will is valid and uncontested, you will settle the estate by filing the proper papers with the probate court. You usually have to provide the court with copies of notices to concerned parties, tax returns, and bills that you have paid. You will also have to provide evidence of distribution of the remaining assets, including signed receipts from the beneficiaries.

After the court recognizes that the probate process has been completed, you will be released from your duties and any further responsibility as personal representative.

No matter how simple or complex an estate is, settling it involves tracking many details and following a specific timeline. Here is a short guide to the proceedings, although you may have more or fewer duties, and your attorney may perform some services, if needed:

- Find the deceased person's will.

- Obtain a lawyer.

- File an application to appear before the probate court, or have your lawyer file one.

- Notify the beneficiaries that the probate process has begun.

- Place a public notice to creditors and mail or personally deliver notices to each known creditor.

- Notify the post office, utilities, banks, and credit card companies of the person's death.

- Collect debts owed to the estate.

- Check with the deceased person's employer for unpaid salary, insurance, and other benefits.

- Take inventory of all assets and have them appraised if necessary.

- File for social security, civil service, or veteran's benefits; life insurance; city, state, and federal tax returns; and state and federal estate-tax returns.

- Make payments for valid claims against the estate.

- Distribute assets to beneficiaries.

- File papers that settle the estate and end your service.

For your own protection, keep a copy of all records for at least two years. Check with legal counsel to find out whether a longer period of time is recommended. Always keep in mind that you can seek guidance from professionals whenever you need help.

Using written agreements will also protect you, and you should obtain written consent from beneficiaries if you change investments. You also may ask beneficiaries to sign a release or consent form to discharge you from liability as long as they are aware of all relevant facts. A court order can protect you from future liability for a particular action. To get such an order, you must present your action to the court, which will decide if it is necessary and beneficial for the estate.

CASE STUDY: KNOW THE JOB

Law Offices of James N. Reyer, P.A.
5301 North Federal Highway, Suite 130
Boca Raton, FL 33487
Phone: (561) 241-9003
Fax: (561) 988-9892

People are often thrust into the role of personal representative or trustee without understanding their true responsibilities. Hire a competent attorney and accountant to see you through the process. You are liable for any mistakes or improper dealings.

Using an attorney and accountant will help you avoid this potential liability. It is their job to protect and advise you on what to do at every step of the administrative process. Nonetheless, it is your role to determine what assets were left by the deceased person and who the beneficiaries are, make sure all assets are protected, pay all outstanding bills, seek out creditors of the estate, and make sure that, at the end of the process, every beneficiary has received a proper share.

Every estate will have disgruntled beneficiaries. When it comes to money, many people feel that a deceased person's will does not reflect what they believe they were entitled to receive or what they had been promised. The true question is not whether beneficiaries complain, but what their rights may be. An unhappy beneficiary is left with only one choice: contest the will. To do this, the beneficiary would have to show that the deceased person was not competent when he or she signed the will, was subject to fraud, or was under influence or duress. This is a very difficult threshold to meet. A competent estate-planning attorney will make sure that any will document meets or exceeds required legal standards.

As a personal representative or trustee, you have a fiduciary duty to the beneficiaries to make sure that all assets are preserved, the value of the estate is not improperly diminished, all creditor claims and taxes are paid, and all beneficiaries receive their proper portions of the estate. If you act improperly, you would be liable to a beneficiary or creditor.

Fees

How should fees for your services, if any, be paid out, and what are the legal and moral obligations involved? In all cases, personal representatives are entitled to reasonable compensation for their services. Time spent can be minimal for a small estate, or can take many hours if the estate has multifaceted concerns. In every case, the fees would be different.

You may find it difficult to decide what to charge for your services. A good place to start is to check state law where the estate is probated. Look for any standard fixed fees and check with county offices to find out about local rules or customs concerning representatives overseeing an estate.

Banking and trust institutions often advertise fixed-fee schedules, but you can negotiate a lower amount if the estate exceeds $1 million. Such negotiations are often made between a potential personal representative and the person interested in naming the bank as a representative of the estate in a will. Qualified estate attorneys also may be knowledgeable about negotiating these fees. Everyone will know that representatives are entitled to reasonable compensation for their work during the process.

An estate's size or complexity or its number of assets does not necessarily determine the fee amount for your services as a personal representative. The type of work involved, the time spent handling the estate, the various problems, your competence and professionalism, and the satisfaction of the beneficiaries are other factors to consider when setting a fee.

Say, for example, you are handling an estate with a value of $500,000, consisting of a free-and-clear home and all assets within the home. Your job as executor, according to the instructions in a will, might be to put the house up for sale and hold an estate sale to sell the major items within the home, depending on what the beneficiaries are entitled to inherit. You sell the home within a reasonable amount of time, sell the assets, pay the necessary fees and commissions, and distribute the remaining funds among the beneficiaries.

Someone else is handling an estate with a value of $500,000, but that estate consists of a home and a small business. The beneficiaries have not decided whether to sell the house or use it as a rental property, and they have not decided what to do about the business since it was not stipulated in the will and was left up to the beneficiaries' desires. The executor will talk with the heirs about the best course of action and make decisions about the business and home. The executor then has to oversee the business dealings and make sure the business and/or home is sold at the proper value. The executor also handles accounting and financial matters with the court, and then distributes the proceeds to the beneficiaries in the proper and legal way.

In your case, you would have been very fortunate. The time you spent handling the estate would have been minimal, as the deceased person's wishes were specified in the will. The other person might not have been so lucky, spending a lot of time — and sometimes being under pressure — to perform the duties correctly. The time spent and the quality of the executor's performance would be large factors in determining the fees owed for services.

That is why keeping a detailed record of the time spent, services rendered, and expenses paid on behalf of the estate is extremely important and valuable to you as a personal representative. A good way to keep track is by informing the beneficiaries step-by-step about what is going on and providing them with receipts for any services performed.

You may also want to negotiate and settle on the fee with every-one involved to avoid any confusion or difficulties later. When expecting a large amount of funds or assets, beneficiaries might have already planned what to do with their windfall. They could be in for a surprise when fees are taken out of their share. If you warn them ahead of time what certain services cost and tell them on a regular basis as you perform each duty, they will have a more realistic idea of what to expect.

At any rate, dealing with this issue early avoids questions later on and makes it easier to handle during the process. It may also let the beneficiaries know what you, as the personal representative, have to do to put the estate and assets in order.

If you are a member of the family as well as a personal representative, you should be aware of the good and bad sides of your dual role. On the positive side, you have inside information and know how other family members view certain situations. Even so, all families have their minor disagreements and battles, no matter how close they are. Your relatives may resent the fees you are receiving for your duties, so this makes keeping records and receipts and letting them know what tasks are involved all the more productive. On the other hand, you are also a beneficiary and may have an advantage in not taking a personal representative's fee, which is taxable — sometimes at a high rate. It might be better to forget about the fee and take the proceeds from the estate because you are dealing with family matters.

Fees can be a little more difficult when co-personal representatives are involved. The fees may be divided equally or, in some states, each personal representative can receive a full fee. When a bank or trust company is a co-personal representative, state laws or the court sometimes award it a higher percentage of a fee.

Family members and close friends may serve as a personal representative or estate trustee without taking compensation. Probate courts, however, have traditionally allowed any person to charge for his or her services during estate transition matters. When banks and trust companies are asked to act as personal representatives or estate trustees, they usually request that the will make a fee agreement clear. A deceased person may specify in the will the fee amount for any personal representative, which can help prevent future conflict.

The courts in estate matters often develop a scale of charges so that personal representatives can determine the amount of compensation they are likely to receive with some precision. This scale is usually based on a percentage of the value of property in the estate.

Also, the law and the courts often allow a certain percentage for capital receipts, in which a personal representative gathers assets of the estate; on capital disbursements in distributing property to beneficiaries; and on revenue receipts when the personal representative receives income, such as bank interest. When the estate is not distributed immediately, an annual care and management fee may be imposed on the gross value of the estate.

Probate courts often follow established guidelines when setting a fair and reasonable fee, based on factors such as the size of the estate, the actual care and responsibility involved, the time occupied in performing duties, the skill and ability shown, and the success and results of the administration of the estate.

CHAPTER 2

The Personal Representative

A close friend, relative, or associate may ask you to accept the honorable role of personal representative (executor or executrix) to represent his or her wishes. If the deceased person does not have a will, the probate court will appoint a personal representative (administrator or administratrix), often a surviving spouse, the oldest child, or another close relative. The court could also appoint someone unknown to the deceased person or even appoint an institution if the family members are in conflict.

The Selection

Personal representatives act in place of the deceased person to distribute assets and property among beneficiaries. So, you are stepping into the deceased person's shoes and operating the estate as he or she would have. Before you assume these responsibilities, you should consider the time and effort that goes into the job of being a replacement figure.

Do not worry if you do not know about financial or other matters facing the estate. You can learn the details of tasks you will be handling. If you have sound values and you always try to keep the interests of the deceased person and the beneficiaries in mind, the rest should come naturally.

The psychological side of dealing with an estate is as important as the financial matters. Those who are considering naming an executor and those who are considering taking on the job should be aware of the skills and care involved. As the estate's personal representative, it is important for you to avoid any potential difficulties with the beneficiaries. Problems may arise if you do not properly communicate and discuss decisions with the heirs.

You might be fully confident and aware of what you are doing, but might fail to consider the beneficiaries while you perform administrative duties. You must take charge and perform the duties the deceased person would perform, but it sometimes may be difficult to judge what that person would have wanted. Family members and beneficiaries can often help you decide the appropriate course of action. This will help you perform the necessary administrative functions in the most efficient way to help bring about the eventual settlement of the estate.

You are standing in place of the deceased person, but the beneficiaries may not always look at it that way. If you perform the functions that you understand were what the deceased person wanted but do not discuss it with the beneficiaries or consider their interests, they will certainly not treat you as they would have treated the deceased person. Any kind of friction that results could lead to more legal headaches and lawsuits.

It is also important for you to act according to the deceased person's wishes in disbursing the estate's assets in a reasonable fashion. A son or daughter may request that you release a certain amount of funds for education, transportation, or job-related purposes. You might believe the child is entitled to a distribution, but the amount requested is too high for the stated purpose, which could be accomplished with fewer funds from the estate. As long as your decision is thought out and reasonable, the court would support it if the beneficiary takes any legal action.

You must use similar methods to reach decisions about selling assets. Give consideration to beneficiaries who may have a stake in those particular assets. Consulting with them and letting them participate in the decision helps relieve any tension that might arise. Sales of investment or property also depend on the ages of the beneficiaries, their personal financial standing, and their desires. You are acting for the deceased person on behalf of the beneficiaries, and you must make any decision in their best interest for the value of the estate.

Aside from knowing or learning about financial matters, knowledge of the estate itself is important. Each beneficiary may have specific needs. It helps, of course, if you are part of the family or close to the family and also understand estate matters, such as investments or businesses once owned by the deceased person. If you are outside the family, you should familiarize yourself with the assets and property of the estate to help you deal with the beneficiaries' wants and needs.

The beneficiaries may be any age, and their needs may vary widely. You might have to stay focused on the different educational or health-related matters a child has to face, or you might be dealing with the day-to-day financial needs of an elderly person. Knowledge of these personal matters is helpful when performing the job of a personal representative.

Likewise, people who consider naming a particular person as an executor should be certain that the person is willing to take on this important role. Anyone named as executor in a will can decline the position, so it is a good idea to discuss your wishes with the person you want to handle your estate. It is also important that the potential executor be aware of the duties required and what it takes to perform those activities. Also, be sure the person you choose is aware of your wishes regarding funeral and burial arrangements.

If you are in the process of selecting an executor for your estate, there are other points to take into account. Trustworthiness should be at the top of your list. Your executor should be someone who would agree with your wishes and understand how you want your property and assets to be disbursed.

Being capable of performing the duties required of an executor is equally important. This is especially key if you have a large estate with complexities that require the advice of a professional, in which case hiring a legal adviser, accountant, or trust company as your executor may be more appropriate.

Someone whom you trust, but who is outside of the family, could make a good executor if you anticipate problems or conflicts among your heirs. Your executor should be someone you anticipate would outlive you, and who lives nearby and can handle the duties of the estate promptly.

You might wish to appoint an alternate executor in case your primary choice is later unable or unwilling to perform the task.

In the process of appointing an executor or considering the position, the location of the estate is important. You might want a close relative to act as your executor, but this might not be the best idea if that person lives far away from the estate property and the beneficiaries. At times, it could be better to select someone who is trustworthy and not necessarily a family member, but who happens to live nearby. A close relative who lives far away may have the best interest of the beneficiaries in mind, but might not be able to accomplish the day-to-day functions of the estate. A good idea in that situation would be to select an outside, trustworthy personal representative while appointing the nearby relative as "guardian of the person" in the case of children, or "guardian of the property." That way, the legal process can continue and the relative can keep a close watch over the beneficiaries' interests.

Competence and Experience

If you have been selected as a personal representative or are the closest heir, you do not have to be knowledgeable in all aspects of estate matters. However, you must have the best interest of the estate in mind and choose qualified professionals, such as banks, attorneys, and financial advisers, to help you if necessary. Competence plays an important role in avoiding disastrous settlements or mistakes. Knowledge of financial matters and management also plays a key role.

A competent person can analyze affairs quickly under a variety of circumstances, determine the best course of action to take, and get assistance when needed anywhere along the way.

When someone is selecting an executor for his or her estate, he or she does not always consider competence, although an outside observer might think it would be a critical factor. This factor can be easily overlooked because emotional issues often take precedence when handling family affairs. A person may choose a family member, such as a spouse or eldest child, as executor simply because of their relationship. This person could be inept when it comes to financial matters, however, throwing the estate into chaos without intending to do so. This potential disaster is made worse because it also could cause a conflict among family members even though the related executor has their best interests at heart.

Just because you are aware of family wishes and the surroundings of the estate does not automatically qualify you as a competent executor. The best and the brightest may lack the necessary talents to handle a loved one's estate. If you have not had experience in making major decisions, you may not have what it takes to represent a relative's estate, no matter how intelligent you are. If you are drawing up a will, consider this when appointing an executor, and the person offered such an opportunity should be certain he or she is competent enough to take on the project.

Banks and trust companies all have professional people with years of experience handling each area of an estate. They have many departments that can supervise the various aspects of assets and property. They know the details involved in all matters of inheritance. It makes sense to appoint an executor who has a variety of experience in similar situations. Depending on the size of the estate, having someone with accounting or financial experience to oversee it offers security for everyone involved.

Personal representatives of smaller estates can succeed with a bit less experience as long as they are wise enough to use professionals when necessary. No matter what you know, if you have the willingness and time to learn, the knowledge to contact the right people, and a desire to provide help to the fullest of your ability, you can do a great job in administering an estate.

A good place to start for anyone without much experience in the area of estate management is to talk to a qualified estate attorney. This consultation, along with knowledge of the estate itself and family matters and concerns, can be of value in pointing you in the right direction during the entire process. The deceased person's will could very well mention or recommend the name of an attorney. It is a good idea for anyone preparing a will to include this information if he or she knows a qualified attorney. Knowing that the beneficiaries will have an experienced and competent person on hand will provide peace of mind.

A good attorney is always there when needed for the personal representative who is not familiar with the steps necessary for the probate process and estate matters. It is like having an assistant on hand during difficult times. In most states, the personal representative can make the final decision in appointing an attorney for the estate. You also have the right to choose another attorney if you are unhappy with the one who drew up the will. However, it is recommended that you stick with the counsel named by the deceased person in a will. Before even beginning to handle the estate, talk openly with the attorney to get information on legal fees and ask questions about the process so you feel more comfortable with it.

Running a Deceased Person's Business

As the estate's personal representative, you may be in charge of the deceased person's business on an interim basis. You must decide whether to continue or terminate the business according to the deceased person's desires or your best judgment. If the business is a partnership, you may have to step in to do what you were instructed, or transfer the business to the surviving partner, depending on the circumstances dictated by the partnership.

Having a business to handle can be a blessing or a curse when it comes to estate matters. Sometimes you can handle it simply — it can even help the estate financially in the end.

At other times it can be difficult, especially if the deceased person's desires have not been specified. If the deceased person has given written instructions on how to dispose of the business, you will have fewer choices to make, and it simplifies the process. Some business partnerships have buy/sell agreements where, if one owner dies, the partner has permission to sell the other's portion of the business and buy it, thereby presenting an easy transition through right of survivorship. The estate may receive payment from the sale. Sometimes, business partners may hold life insurance on the other partner and can pay proceeds from the policy to buy the partner's business interests from the estate.

It is another story, however, if no agreements were made, meaning you have to step into the shoes of the deceased person temporarily as a business owner. It is then up to you whether to continue the business or terminate it. A deceased person may have left instructions to continue the business, which you would oversee until the proper disbursements are settled. You would have to watch over the business until your duty as personal representative ended, but you also would not have to spend time trying to sell the business at the "correct" price to satisfy the interest of beneficiaries. Left with no instructions, you most likely would seek the probate court's approval in matters relating to the business, whether to keep it going or sell it. This can be a difficult situation if you do not have the expertise to handle a business, especially a particular enterprise you may know nothing about. A business owner preparing a will should keep this in mind when appointing an executor. A person considering taking on an estate that includes a business should have some business sense, or at least know whom to go to for advice.

That is not to say that an estate's personal representative must be an expert in the deceased person's business. Many professional personal representatives may handle establishments they were not involved with before, but they often have some experience in the area and know where to turn whenever they need professional advice. They may have handled similar estates in the past. More generally, a personal representative might need only management experience in order to take on the details and difficulties of handling any business.

The same is true when selecting an executor to handle an estate that has many investments. Obviously, a person with experience in the financial field would be a tremendous asset in this situation. Some investment knowledge, however, is helpful in serving as personal representative of any estate.

Some people choose banking or trust companies to handle either all or part of their estates. They may have a bank handle their investments, with a co-personal representative taking care of the remaining estate. Financial institutions can easily handle investments securely because they have experience in the financial market. Investment funds can grow at a safe and comfortable pace while the rest of the estate proceedings take place.

People who are successful investors may have close contact with financial advisers and brokers they can trust. They may designate these professionals as advisers for the estate's personal representative.

Of course, if you are the executor and do not have the expertise to handle investments, you should seek the services of reputable financial advisers to answer questions and keep the deceased person's investments safe. Do not think you can just leave the investments alone. During uncertain times, stocks can rise or fall, and you would risk losing money for the estate if you just pushed investment funds to the side. A financial adviser or broker can keep the investment portfolio at healthy growth levels.

Qualities to Look for in a Financial Advisor

FINANCIAL ADVISOR FILES

Make sure the potential candidate is a designated Certified Financial Planner (CFP). This means that he or she has had at least three years of experience in the field, and has had extensive coursework and passed an in-depth financial exam. Other certifications can include: Certified Public Account (CPA), Chartered Financial Analyst (CFA), and Chartered Life Underwriter (CLU), among others.

Run your own background check on the candidate. Ask for both sections of their Form ADV, which registers him or her with the Securities and Exchange Commission (SEC). The first part lets you know whether they have had run-ins with other clients. The second part tells you what services they provide and how much those services cost, as well as investment strategies.

Choose someone you can connect with. Taking part in the estate of a deceased loved one can be a taxing experience, so comfort is key in terms of how you feel with the financial advisor and his or her methods and approach.

Do You Want to Be a Personal Representative?

Do you feel you would make the right decisions? Do you have the time and knowledge to serve? You also have to consider location — whether or not you are near the estate's probate court and majority of assets. If you are appointed as a personal representative, you do not have to accept the position if the responsibility is too much for you to take on, or if the decision would not be in the best interest of the beneficiaries and the deceased person's intentions.

The duties and responsibilities of a personal representative require a considerable amount of time and effort, knowledge in some areas, and care and concern for people who will be depending on you. The average estate can take six to nine months to settle, perhaps longer. Larger estates can take two or more years, and can be quite taxing if many disputes and lawsuits arise. If you do not have the time, that may be a reason to avoid being a personal representative. You could also consider having banks, trusts, and other co-personal representatives or professionals step in to help when necessary. If you are choosing an executor, take into consideration that person's ability to be impartial and objective when dealing with your beneficiaries.

Likewise, potential personal representatives should be aware of the conflicts that could arise among beneficiaries. They also need to remember to stay out of these conflicts as much as possible, arriving at the proper conclusions that satisfy the deceased person's wishes. When discussing your role as personal representative with the person who is asking to assign you, make sure steps are taken in advance to avoid as many conflicts as possible. Also, ask about co-personal representatives who can play vital roles in helping you administer the estate, whether they are banking institutions or professionals.

CHAPTER 3

The Trustee

A property owner may choose a trustee before death to manage the estate, prepare the proper disbursement of assets, or handle finances for minor children or incapacitated heirs. The trustee may be a knowledgeable individual, family member, bank, or trust company. The deceased person might have selected a family member to act as trustee, but chose a bank or trust company to handle the property for a spouse or children. The trustee must act in accordance with the terms of the trust and with legal codes.

What is a Trust?

A trust is a legal relationship that allows a person to hold money or other property that the grantor, or creator of the trust, transfers to the trust for the benefit of one or more beneficiaries. As trustee, you hold legal title to the property, but must use it only for the benefit of the beneficiaries. There are a variety of trust types, including trusts that end in death, trusts that go on after death to protect and provide for beneficiaries, trusts created for tax purposes, children's trusts, life insurance trusts, and charitable trusts.

Trusts can be divided into two general categories: revocable and irrevocable. The grantor can alter or terminate a revocable trust. The irrevocable trust, in most cases, cannot be altered or terminated, except by court order. The courts will order this only if there is fraud, if there is proof of undue influence when the trust was established, or if a technical change needs to be made that does not adversely affect the interests of the beneficiaries or the trust's purposes.

The trust document or agreement spells out written instructions on how assets are to be managed or invested, as well as who will receive any income or assets from the trust, how those allocations are distributed, and when the income or assets are paid.

A trust fund is a legal relationship or contract between the trustee — either a person or trust company — and the grantor to hold property for the benefit of the beneficiaries. The trust may include property, money, stocks, bonds, businesses, and other assets. The grantor and beneficiaries may use it to avoid future legal costs, including avoiding probate and resolving any issues during distributions of the trust. As trustee, you will handle certain assets in accordance with the grantor's wishes as stipulated in the trust agreement, and you will make assets available to the beneficiaries when the proper time comes. This can occur during the existence of the trust or when it ends upon the grantor's death and disbursements are completed.

Although you hold the legal title to the property in the trust, the beneficiaries have the right to benefit from the property as stated in the trust agreement. The grantor can still retain control of the property if a revocable trust is set up with the grantor also listed as the trustee. In this way, the grantor may add to the trust, or sell or distribute anything from the trust.

State laws govern trusts, so whether the trust includes property or various assets, rules of the state where the grantor created the trust will apply. People who have residences in more than one state might choose to name the state they would prefer to control the assets when distribution takes place.

Trusts are, in a way, like invisible units that do not have an actual location. Property is simply owned by the particular trust.

When a person creates a trust and transfers the property to you as trustee to manage it, you will manage all property and assets for the beneficiaries according to the written terms of the trust document. The grantor might do this to have a qualified person deal with estate planning, tax, and asset-management issues. The trust often addresses estate-planning matters, such as tax savings, avoiding probate, protecting family members, and handling how and when to distribute assets to named beneficiaries.

As trustee, you can make investments, manage the property, and administer the estate because you hold the legal title to the property in the trust. However, the property and income produced from it remains in the hands of the beneficiaries.

You are merely there to safeguard, invest, and pay out any assets, which means any income or capital obtained from those assets.

Administering a trust is an obligation with a variable duration. You can be a trustee for a few years or many years. A trust can last several generations and be administered by several trustees along the way. You also may have co-trustees that can include bank and trust companies or individuals.

The beneficiaries will receive any income from the trust as stipulated by the trust agreement, which may spell out certain terms and conditions that may pertain to the age of the beneficiaries. Primary beneficiaries are the first people to receive distributions from the trust. For instance, a parent may receive income throughout his or her life until death. At that point, a child might receive what remains of the trust. The child would be called the remainderman.

A living trust, which is set up during the grantor's lifetime, may hold assets that the grantor contributed during his or her lifetime, or it could hold assets owned at death.

A trust created under a will is a testamentary trust. The grantor retains all rights to the property during his or her lifetime, but assets pass from the will into the trust at the time of death. The trust is then passed on to the beneficiaries according to the terms of the will and trust. A testamentary trust helps cut down on paperwork because the will and the trust are both in the same document. A living trust and will require two separate documents. A testamentary trust might not be valid, however, if the will is not probated and is successfully challenged in court. The grantor still owns the assets and income in a testamentary trust, making it subject to income and estate taxes.

Trusts: An Example

A trust is a legal arrangement that involves the transfer of property from the original owner to a person or a company for the purpose of holding and maintaining the property until it is handed over to the beneficiary — the individual or institution designated to receive the property.

It seems straightforward enough, until you get into the many legal terms, people, laws, and taxes that go into the creation of a trust. With many interchangeable terms, some of which are as confusing as the Greek or Roman terms from which they originated, a list of who is who and what is what is helpful.

The following situation will assist you with recognizing the roles each person plays in a trust.

People: Aunt Tara wants to set up a trust for her house so that her niece, Betsy, will have a place to set up her veterinary clinic after she finishes her education. However, she does not know when Betsy will graduate, so she wants her grandson Charles to take care of the place if she — Aunt Tara — dies. In case something happens to Charles, his wife, Kim, will take on that responsibility.

- **Trustor** (Aunt Tara): The person who sets up the trust. Other names commonly used are creator, donor, settlor, or grantor.

- **Beneficiary** (Betsy): The individual(s) or group(s) that will receive the property in the trust. This can be a single person, a group of people, one group, several groups, or a combination of any of these.

- **Trustee** (Charles): The person or company that will oversee or manage the trust once it is established. This person (or group) will make sure the property in the trust is safe and in good order until it is turned over to the beneficiary. This includes paying any taxes, performing repairs, or anything else an owner would do. The trustee is obligated to carry out the terms of the trust and can be paid for this effort if terms for this are included in the trust language.

- **Successor trustee** (Kim): Someone who will step in if the primary trustee is unable to serve or cannot continue to manage

manage the trust. This person will have the same legal obligations for managing the trust as the original trustee, should the successor assume the management responsibilities.

The individual or company designated to serve as trustee carries a significant amount of responsibility and needs to be someone you trust implicitly. The potential for a conflict of interest or being swayed by the temptation to do something inappropriate — such as stealing from the trust or neglecting the work — needs to be considered. Putting language in the trust documents that spells out the responsibilities of the trustees is essential, and creating a mechanism or oversight and removal will also prevent heirs from losing what is supposed to be theirs.

Things and strings: Aunt Tara's house sits on four acres of land with an outbuilding to store the lawn tractor and other equipment. Over the years, she sold off the other 12 acres, so she invested the money into a mutual fund. Aunt Tara had her lawyer set up a trust fund that gives Betsy the interest from the mutual fund to pay tuition when it is due in the fall, but Aunt Tara's mutual fund will not go to Betsy until she graduates from college. The house in the care of Charles will also go to Betsy after she graduates.

- **Property**: Anything you want to give to other people, also referred to as principal. There are all kinds of legal terms for the "stuff" you own, and you have to make sure you use the right words to identify everything from money in a safe or checking account to a rocking chair or commemorative baseball. This can be real property or real estate (10-acre farm), tangible personal property (the things you can touch, such as a lawn tractor and other equipment), or intangible personal property (financial assets, such as certificates of deposit).

- **Trust agreement**: The legal document that spells out the terms of a trust, including the people and conditions, as well as the rules that must be followed. Some are state or federal laws, and others are specific conditions (trust fund).

- **Funding a trust**: The placement of property in a trust; that same property will be called trust principal once it is under the auspices of the trust agreement.

- **Provisions**: The clauses that spell out how you want your wishes carried out. Distribution provisions will identify to whom the income will be given and the frequency of those distributions (pay tuition when it is due in the fall). Special provisions encompass all requirements that are unique to the beneficiary or the assets (graduates from college).

- **Legal title**: This gives the trustee ownership of the property in the trust for the duration of the trustee's responsibility (house in Charles's care).

- **Beneficial title**: Also known as Equitable Title, this is the right of the person or institution to take possession of or benefit from the property in the trust (goes to Betsy).

Benefits of a Trust

A trust's grantor may believe a beneficiary is unable to manage, invest, or handle the responsibility of an outright gift. The trust can postpone full ownership until the beneficiary is ready. A trust:

- Gives the grantor better control over disbursements.
- Allows assets to be protected from the claims of creditors.
- Provides equality in treatment for children and grandchildren.
- Avoids probate and reduces the possibility of a contested will.
- Keeps details about finances as private as possible.
- Can relieve the grantor of the burden of investing or managing property.

Privacy or protection may play a major role in why people set up trusts. The instructions in a will can be made public, especially during cases when the will is contested. A trust may also be an ideal way to conserve funds for a person who is incapable of handling money. The trustee may be in a better position to disburse funds in the way the trust document originally instructed.

Trusts are even beneficial for companies, which often set them up for pension plans or use them as investments for benefits going to employees and their dependents. Trusts also may be used to protect a person from future creditors. The grantor can benefit from the trust without actually owning the assets because the trustee handles the ownership and the grantor remains anonymous.

A trust can reduce the probability of a contested will in many states by keeping the trust property outside of probate. It also avoids the expense involved in probate.

Children can benefit immensely from trusts, especially if they are physically or emotionally handicapped or if they are not stable enough yet to handle finances. Full ownership of the trust does not usually occur until the child reaches maturity or is deemed sufficiently able to handle property and income. The grantor may decide when it is the correct time for the child to receive ownership. Some grantors set aside the interest from trust assets to go to their children and have the remaining principal go to charities.

Trusts also boost the security of the estate's finances and property. The grantor may determine when assets should be disbursed, and what beneficiaries receive those assets. A trust helps prevent beneficiaries from disposing of certain items, including property and businesses, to people outside the family.

Because the trust is protected from claims of creditors, when the grantor uses an irrevocable trust and the children and grandchildren are treated as equal beneficiaries, the grantor maintains complete control over the trust while avoiding any unnecessary activities, such as management or investment, which the trustee will handle.

Revocable trusts are used to reduce legal fees that often arise, sometimes substantially, from probate. This may not be the case with small trusts that can be handled alone, according to the grantor's wishes. Even in that case, trustees should consult with qualified attorneys concerning all estate matters, including federal estate-tax returns and allocations of trust assets that will affect beneficiaries in the future.

Trustees, grantors, and beneficiaries also benefit when trust assets can be used for legal and financial fees, which can be tax-deductible. Beneficiaries may also receive shares of trust assets free of income tax.

The flexibility of trusts is another benefit. For example, they can help provide for children, particularly those who are handicapped and whose needs may change over time. That is why the grantor should choose the right trustee, someone who knows the family's needs and affairs, to handle the trust. This is also true when dealing with a family business or investments.

Setting up a trust can help many people sleep well at night, knowing the future is planned and settled. Still, consulting with a knowledgeable attorney is the first important step in selecting a trustee.

Types of Trusts

The following is a list of the different types of trusts:

- **Burial trust**: Provides the funds necessary to cover the cost of your burial or cremation arrangements. This can be a revocable trust, but it becomes irrevocable after your death and cannot be used for anything else.

- **Charitable trust**: Offers the benefits of tax-free gifts for the donor. A charitable remainder trust gives gifts of interest income that are paid to specific beneficiaries, such as your spouse, for a specific period of time; at the end of that time period, a charity receives whatever is left in the trust. A charitable lead trust, or a front trust, gives the charity a specific gift before all other beneficiaries receive anything. These are both split-interest trusts. Split-interest trusts make distributions to both charitable and non-charitable beneficiaries, while providing tax benefits to their donor.

- **Crummey trust**: An exceedingly complicated trust normally set up in conjunction with an irrevocable life insurance trust to make the payments for a life insurance policy. This is the kind of trust that requires an estate-planning attorney to create.

- **Educational trust**: This is a kind of protective trust that sets aside money specifically for education-related expenses, such as tuition or training fees, books, or supplies. These trusts regularly include provisions to stop payments if the student drops out of school or flunks many classes.

- **Generation-skipping transfer trust (GSTT)**: A tax-saving trust designed to benefit multiple generations after you are gone.

- **Grantor-retained trusts**: These are irrevocable and non-charitable, which means they cannot be changed and the beneficiary is not a charity. There are three common types: A Grantor-Retained Annuity Trust (GRAT) gives a fixed amount of money at predetermined times, often at regularly scheduled intervals; a Grantor-Retained Unit Trust (GRUT) pays a specific percentage to the beneficiary; and a Grantor-Retained Incomes Trust

(GRIT) designates specific people to receive certain property, such as stocks or a house, but the income or use of the property stays with you until your death.

- **Living trust**: Created while you are still alive, this trust allows you to be the grantor, trustee, and beneficiary, if you choose.

- **Marital dedication trust**: Puts property into a trust that is exclusively for your spouse, who decides what happens to the property after your death.

- **Minor trust**: A way to give gifts to minors that avoids the gift tax and keeps the property safe until the minor becomes an adult and can take ownership of the trust.

- **QTIP**: A Qualified Terminable Interest Property trust is a marital deduction trust. Instead of your spouse deciding who gets the property after your death, the grantor makes that decision.

- **Spendthrift trust**: A trust that is set up for someone who will not be able to handle their own affairs, i.e., someone who is mentally incompetent or might have financial problems and needs protection from creditors. The beneficiary does not own the property in the trust, just the payments that are made from the trust.

- **Special needs trust**: A support trust for a disabled person under the age of 65 (you or anyone else). This trust makes payments on the beneficiary's behalf, as required by the state as reimbursement. After the beneficiary dies, the property in the trust is paid to other beneficiaries. This trust is designed to protect your property from seizure by the government or a creditor seeking reimbursement.

- **Supplemental needs trust**: A support trust designed to provide income to a handicapped, elderly, or disabled person to supplement their income, but is structured in a way that does not reduce or jeopardize the eligibility of that person to receive public or private benefits. This trust is designed to protect your property from seizure by the government or a creditor seeking reimbursement.

- **Testamentary trust**: Created by the terms of your will after your death.

- **Totten trust**: This is a bank account that, upon your death, immediately passes to the named beneficiary.

How is a Trustee Selected?

As with the role of personal representative, appointment as a trustee is an honor. It means someone believes you can be trusted and are competent enough to be in control of his or her assets for the benefit of the people near and dear to that person. Many people who create trusts do not have the knowledge or understanding about the difficulty of the trustee's job. The trustee's task is to carry out the terms of the trust agreement and manage the assets of an estate. Few people understand what legal responsibilities await the trustee or the difficulties that can arise while the trustee manages the estate.

People may choose a family member or close friend to handle a trust because of their relationship, but they might be better off using more objective guidelines in making a decision that will affect their family for many years to come.

When considering becoming a trustee for someone's estate, remember that many responsibilities are involved. You will become the legal owner of the trust property, while acting on behalf of the beneficiaries who are entitled to all interests and benefits as provided by the trust's grantor.

As the manager and owner of the trust, you may be buying or selling assets, but the income will belong to the beneficiaries, as will the ownership of the assets in time. You are, in a sense, minding the store and making sure all proceeds are handled properly for the people entitled to them. You must stand guard over those proceeds and keep them going to the beneficiaries.

You are expected to sell or buy investments responsibly and effectively, manage all expenses of the estate, use professional advisers when necessary, disburse funds properly to beneficiaries, and keep the beneficiaries informed on a regular basis. Most importantly, you must keep the interests of the beneficiaries above your own.

At times, it may be difficult to manage the trust in the way it was intended. Some beneficiaries may not be completely happy with the trust's intended purposes. You have to follow the trust's instructions, however, regardless of emotional issues. Failure to exercise your responsibility as a trustee can result in legal problems and even lifelong damage down the road. Penalties for inept behavior can include financial loss or jail time if you are not dedicated to honesty and integrity in this highly prestigious position.

Do you have the qualifications to be appointed as a trustee? Some of the characteristics would include honesty and trustworthiness, intelligence, good sense, conscientiousness, availability, fairness, good health, responsibility, financial skills, legal knowledge, communication abilities, patience, and empathy. You will be acting on your own many times without the rigorous regulations that banking and trust professionals must adhere to, so you must be honest when dealing with beneficiaries.

This is no ordinary job; you are in charge and have the responsibility to know how and when to perform certain duties, make good decisions that will affect the beneficiaries, and know who can assist you when you need professional guidance. You will be handling other people's money and must have the good sense to know how to do that properly.

This means keeping accurate records and documenting everything you do concerning the estate. This will be a necessity in case you have to explain your actions in court.

You will have ongoing duties when it comes to investments, tax matters, and the courts. You must be meticulous about accuracy and timeliness in any action or report for the sake of the beneficiaries. With large, complex trusts, you may have to be available to attend meetings, make payments, or deal with emergencies when assets require immediate attention. It is not something you have to stay on top of all the time, but you should be able to keep practical business hours to deal with any matters that arise.

Impartiality is key when dealing with a trust's beneficiaries. You must act fairly in all matters of the estate. You will be called on to look at all sides of an issue and make important decisions. Beneficiaries who need funds for different reasons may approach you. They may all need finances to improve their lives, but you may need to curtail or deny their requests when funds are not sufficient, if the requests are not in line with the trust's provisions, or if one beneficiary needs the money more urgently than another. It is not always easy being fair, but that will be your job as trustee.

You should be in reasonably good health when you take on the responsibility of being a trustee. After all, you are handling an estate that belongs to others who depend on you during this entire period. You will be making important financial decisions that will affect their lives. You should focus on those duties while in the best possible shape.

You should be responsible enough to take blame if things go wrong. Investments may experience losses through no fault of your own. You should be prepared to take financial responsibility and pay back any losses that stem from acts that someone could consider negligent. You may want to purchase bonding and insurance to protect you from any losses that disgruntled beneficiaries may bring to the court. In some states, you are required to provide a bond.

At this point, it might be a good idea to think of the skills you have in financial or legal matters. You will be dealing with laws, accounting, taxes, investments, and other factors in the world of finance. You do not have to be an expert in all of these areas, but you should know various professionals who are skilled in areas you are not familiar with so you can get the assistance you need. Keep in mind when delegating certain powers to others that you are still in charge. You have to keep abreast of all actions they take and know the reasons they are taking them. You remain the supervisor, while others may handle work you cannot perform.

Communication is important in all matters of the estate. It helps to be an effective communicator during your contacts with beneficiaries and professionals. This promotes good relations, which results in smoother operations and better understanding among everyone involved.

During the difficult times of operating the trust, you have to be patient. The trust's beneficiaries are not doing the job you are doing, and they may not fully understand why you take certain actions. At times like this, you should be able to carefully (and patiently) explain what is going on and be empathetic to the beneficiaries' feelings. This could be particularly tough when dealing with beneficiaries who are elderly, not in good health or mental condition, or are suffering from personal problems. The challenge is to keep them calm and comfortable, while building a good rapport that allows you to explain situations in a composed manner.

Above all, you have to remain cheerful no matter how hard it may be during negative periods. Handling some situations with humor can do wonders to reduce friction and tension in your dealings with others, as long as you apply it gently and at the right time.

From the other side, when you as a grantor decide to establish a trust, you will need to do some homework and use thought when considering the selection of the trustee. Sometimes, it is best to name a professional as the trustee, such as a bank representative, trust company, or attorney. At any rate, you should choose a person or persons who can be trusted with this major task. The trustee, after all, will be handling your property and assets, and then distribute them to your beneficiaries.

The trustee must comply with your wishes and terms in the trust agreement. As a trust grantor, you should be looking at all personal and family matters, including investment and business concerns, when choosing someone to run the trust. You most likely will want to choose professional or corporate trustees to handle a trust for properties that are large and complex. Trust companies have many options available for your investment or financial concerns and for tax planning, but at times do not operate on a personal basis and might make investments on your behalf more conservatively. Smaller trusts would not necessarily require professional assistance, and a trustworthy person known to you could manage them.

Another concern is how long you expect the trust to last. A trust fund could carry through several generations. If this is the case, corporate trustees would be better able to handle the trust. Although people administering the trust probably will change over time, large companies can maintain records and keep federal and state requirements up-to-date. Some grantees assign co-trustees to handle various aspects of the trust for long-term funds.

Banking and trust companies most likely will be impartial when it comes to dealing with beneficiaries. However, grantors still may consider choosing non-professionals for economic reasons and because they will be administering small trusts.

CHAPTER 4

The Emotional Side

An estate's personal representative or trustee must understand the grief process that beneficiaries may face when going through the loss of a loved one. The length of the process varies, depending on the passing. For instance, if death is expected as a result of terminal illness, loved ones may have more time to prepare for coping with grief.

The Grieving Process

Whether you are handling estate affairs as an outsider or as a close relative assigned as personal representative, you should understand that beneficiaries have just endured the loss of a loved one in many cases. Aside from dealing with the necessities of financial and property concerns on a regular basis, family members are also going through the trauma and trials of a sudden void in their lives. This can have an enormous impact on their feelings and the decisions that must be made as the legal process gets under way.

When you are both a family member and a personal representative, you will be dealing with deep emotional issues as you juggle the official duties of estate proceedings. Once the initial shock subsides slightly for the family members, the sadness of knowing they will never see this person again will follow. Conflicts and bitterness may arise among the heirs as their emotions go head-to-head with the financial matters.

If you have already been through the loss of a loved one, your experience might help you handle estate affairs in a gentle manner. As a reminder, or for those who do not fully understand the way survivors approach dealing with grief, you should learn about the emotions that run through the average survivor's mind. This will help in your dealings with the beneficiaries, as well as with your job in taking charge of the estate at a crucial time.

Psychologists and bereavement experts generally accept that a person goes through five stages when facing his or her own death or the death of a loved one: denial, anger, bargaining, depression, and, finally, acceptance. These stages are based on the pioneering methods created by the late Dr. Elisabeth Kubler-Ross, author of *On Death & Dying*, in the support and counseling of grief and grieving. Counseling groups, medical centers, and physicians all over the world have adopted these stages and use them in their work.

Dying people often experience these stages, too, and survivors go through the stages both as a loved one is dying and after the death.

Denial

Denial occurs when someone refuses to accept the facts of death or the reality relating to death. It is a defense mechanism and a natural reaction. When death occurs, however, the reality is not easy to avoid indefinitely.

Anger

People facing the possibility of death can become angry with themselves and others for a variety of reasons. This is an emotion that you should be aware of as personal representative because someone who is preparing to die may take the anger out on one or more family members when making estate plans. Any sudden or last-minute change concerning a beneficiary, or even a personal representative or trustee, is an indication of this phase. Anger can have a strong effect on all survivors, interfering with the process of grieving and dealing with estate necessities. If anger is directed at you as the personal representative or trustee, you must do your best to remain objective without responding with your own hostility. Try to understand the grief process that the dying person and survivors are going through.

Bargaining

The bargaining process may involve an attempt to bargain with God or the beyond. This can occur during any crisis, but is particularly the case when facing life or death. For example, if a woman's husband was terminally ill, she might pray, "If he gets better, I promise to give more money to charity."

Depression

This can be a response to accepting the death with an emotional attachment. It also shows that the person is beginning to accept reality along with the sadness and uncertainty that comes with it.

Acceptance

The person finally accepts the circumstances that come with death. The final stage may vary among people as they deal with the situation they face on a personal level. A person experiencing the acceptance of a loved one's death might begin to plan things for the future with a sense of hope, or even think about the deceased person without feeling wrenching pain.

After the loss

According to experts of the grieving process at the University of Texas in Austin, survivors can experience different grief reactions regarding sudden versus predictable loss. Sudden or shocking losses from such events as accidents, crimes, or suicide can be severely traumatic, leaving the survivor with a sense of hopelessness. The family member or close friend is unable to prepare for the loss. This can upset their sense of security and assurance in the regularity and balance of life. Survivors may experience such symptoms as sleep disturbances or nightmares, disturbing thoughts, social isolation, or extreme anxiety after a loss.

Predictable losses, such as those resulting from terminal or lingering illness, sometimes allow a cushion of extra time to prepare, but hardly soften the blow of the loss. These losses are also capable of creating two layers of grief: the grief associated with awaiting the loss and the grief pertaining to the final loss.

Researchers explain that individuals experience the grief process differently. It can be extremely painful at times, and it cannot be rushed. It is important for the survivors to be as patient as possible while experiencing their feelings and other people's individual reactions to the loss. Things get better with support and the passing of time. Holidays, significant dates like birthdays and anniversaries, and other reminders, however, can again spark feelings related to the loss.

Grief counselors advise survivors to take care of themselves, seek support, and talk with others about the feelings they are going through to help cope.

When grieving, it is common to have feelings of sadness or depression. The inability to focus on simple tasks is common, and it is possible to feel irritable or angry with the deceased person or others. Excessive frustration can surface, or you may experience emotional anxiety, nervousness, or fear. You may want to "escape," or you may have feelings of guilt, remorse, ambivalence, and numbness.

The Counseling and Mental Health Center at the University of Texas suggests supporting survivors going through the grieving process by:

- Being a good listener
- Asking about their feelings
- Sitting with them
- Sharing your feelings
- Asking about their loss
- Remembering the loss

- Making telephone calls
- Acknowledging the pain
- Letting them feel sad
- Being available when you can
- Not minimizing the grief
- Talking about your own losses

Grief counselors at the University of Texas point out that people going through the grieving process often may feel isolated and lonely. These feelings can increase as the loss begins to fade for friends who had been providing support for the survivor soon after the death. People with grieving friends may want to show some concern and consideration at this difficult time.

Thinking and Decisions Are Affected

The death may have a lingering emotional impact among the survivors, affecting the way they deal with the estate process. They may experience guilt, loneliness, and resentment, as well as the shock of the sudden change or the financial burdens they may be facing. Personal representatives and trustees should be aware of these emotional changes.

The death of a loved one can be particularly traumatic when that person is the one in charge of family matters, the main source of income for the family, and the one who is the financial and emotional bond for the many fragments of family concerns. In the beginning, this can be as equally shocking as learning of a family member's death because the survivor or survivors discover they are now responsible for the tasks involved in keeping the family fully functioning. The emotional upheaval imposed by the loved one's death now carries over into the day-to-day schedule of handling important affairs that require business and financial knowledge.

If a spouse is left alone to handle these important responsibilities, it can become chaotic and lead to disaster if not properly administered. Losing a spouse has enormous emotional implications. Not only is the surviving spouse hit with sudden legal and financial demands, but he or she is often in the worst possible mental state to look at such matters clearly.

These losses affect older widows and widowers differently. If an older widow has been left with the enormous tasks at hand, the demands of the estate may be particularly daunting. She may have emotional support from extended family and friends, but is still in the vulnerable position of making decisions and choices affecting her personal property, possessions, and her own financial security (in some cases, for the first time in her life). She may lack the experience and knowledge about the subjects facing her and her future, or her health may compromise her ability to cope with estate matters.

Widowers traditionally face somewhat different cultural and emotional challenges. If they have been used to business matters, that aspect of estate management may not be as daunting, but they still have to cope with the emotional aspects of the situation for themselves and their family. These dynamics are usually harder for men than women in our current society. Because men tend not to have the same emotional network as women, they may feel isolated and lonely as a result.

In addition to the surviving spouse, other family members will experience the emotional and riveting effects of a loved one's death. Everyone going through the grieving process will have to face the emotions of sadness, regrets, and "what-ifs." People who have had to deal with a loved one's lingering or terminal illness may experience guilt for feeling temporary relief or even happiness that the person has died. Even in cases when the deceased person had been suffering greatly and is finally at rest, loved ones still feel the person's loss deeply and experience strong emotions following death.

Conflicts About Disbursements

If a deceased person leaves a will, it may have an emotional impact on the survivors and could provoke conflicts about the distributions of property and assets. Beneficiaries are hearing what are perceived to be the deceased person's last thoughts. They may not fully understand these plans.

As executor, you need to be attuned to such emotions and traumas in addition to the legal aspects of the estate. Personal conflicts within an individual and within the family may need attention, at least for a time after the death. You, by the deceased person's appointment, have been put in charge of these issues.

Equally as important as the family's mental and emotional state are the financial burdens and new responsibilities that await many of them for the first time. The survivors may feel they are unable to deal with the weighty matters suddenly thrust before them.

Sometimes, they do not even care because of the overbearing emotions gripping them. At times, your job as personal representative is to keep the person on track, no matter how difficult. You might have to be tough once in a while, but it would most certainly be in the family's best interests.

This is important to keep in mind when bringing up the will, which is often the last communication the loved one is making with the survivors. You have to let people know, using your best legal and interpersonal abilities, that this is the way the deceased person wanted things. If the will's terms anger a survivor, it does not necessarily mean the deceased person was being difficult or upset. Instead, the will reflects the deceased person's thoughts when deciding the best way for the estate to be distributed. For example, you might remind an heir who may have been given less than he or she felt was due that another family member may be in dire need of certain assets because of physical or financial requirements. You also might not have to "explain" anything other than reminding the survivor that the will reflects the deceased person's wishes. Always remember that you are dealing with people in vulnerable positions. The way they think is not necessarily the normal way they operate. You sometimes will have to make decisions for them, and they probably will be grateful for it in time.

As personal representative or trustee, this is a good time to let the survivors participate in the estate as much as possible. It will make them feel the importance of being a family member, as well as help them understand the complex issues their loved one may have been going through. You are not necessarily in total control of the estate and should lend an ear to the beneficiaries to take into consideration the thoughts and emotions with which they are struggling. This will be helpful to everyone involved. It may also help relieve the depression of the beneficiaries amid the grieving process.

The more the family members are involved in the estate, the more they will have contact with each other. This can help prevent conflicts that may arise during the distribution of property and assets.

CHAPTER 5

The Estate Dream Team

A s a personal representative or trustee, you will most likely need the help of advisers, professionals, and possibly other co-personal representatives, no matter how knowledgeable you are in estate management. You will need financial, accounting, real estate, emotional, and legal advice when performing your duties. Whether you are a novice or an experienced manager, professional experts are available to give you help.

Attorneys

You will face legal and tax issues related to the estate. An estate lawyer can answer all your questions and ensure the timely preparation and filing of forms and information. The attorney can answer questions about financial holdings, handling a business, or proper disbursements.

If the deceased person did not have a will and the court has appointed you as administrator, you will have the full authority to select an attorney you believe can best help you handle the estate.

If you are appointed by a will, the deceased person may have specified that you use a certain attorney. Many states, however, do not consider this binding; rather, it is merely a suggestion. You have the freedom to choose the attorney who can provide the most effective advice for estate matters. After all, you are the one who is accountable for all matters facing the estate and who has to work with the attorney.

The attorney is a vital part of the estate team. Naturally, you will be able to handle many of the routine decisions affecting the estate, but when dealing with financial, legal, property, and beneficiary issues, the attorney can spell out the pros, cons, and legal necessities of any decision. Even so, you can still be held responsible if you follow bad advice given by attorneys. If you do not have a good feeling about a particular attorney's advice, you should seek out another legal adviser.

When choosing an attorney in the beginning of the probate process, you might want to consult with two or three attorneys to get an idea about their expertise and fees. Most attorneys provide a free initial consultation. They can also discuss the basics of their services during a meeting, but they might charge you for further consultation and are entitled to those fees.

You should not choose an attorney based solely on fees. An attorney's knowledge and expertise may be more important in handling certain estates. This, in turn, could save thousands of dollars in the end when an experienced attorney knows how to avoid possible mistakes and can provide advice on financial and tax matters. Many states certify attorneys as estate and trust specialists. Find out if such specialists are available in your area by contacting your state bar association for a list.

Choosing the Right Attorney

ATTORNEY FILES

You should look for these qualities in the attorney you retain:

- Look for an attorney who specializes in estate planning. What experience does he or she have that will serve your needs? What amount of dedication and time can your attorney give you? Ask about the person's legal experience in your area and with people whose financial situation is similar to yours.

- Choose an estate-planning attorney who is certified in your state (if this is an option in your state).

- Can you trust the attorney? You want someone that you feel has your best interests at heart and who is working for you. You should like the person, as you will be dealing with him or her for some time to come.

Insurance Agents

Insurance agents offer fast and free help regarding policies held by the deceased person. You can use life insurance policies to pay off expenses and debts for the estate. You may be able to borrow cash on behalf of the estate from the people who received the insurance, or sell them estate assets in exchange for cash. You will have to follow certain court procedures in doing this. As the personal representative, you may also be the recipient of life insurance on behalf of the estate.

The agency or agent who provided a deceased person's life insurance policy can take care of matters quickly when you provide them with a death certificate, claim form, or a copy of the policy itself.

When planning your estate, keep your life insurance policies in a safe, secure place that surviving family members or beneficiaries can find easily, such as a fireproof metal case.

When selecting an insurance agent or company, choose one that is reputable, has many estate and trust clients, and has been in the business for some time.

Personal representatives should consult with insurance agents and companies to inquire about the best way to use insurance resources for the estate's benefit. A good agent may suggest new insurance needs for the estate to help you best serve the beneficiaries.

Choosing the Right Insurance Agent

INSURANCE AGENT FILES

You should look for these qualities in the agent you retain:

- Ask for a referral for a good insurance agent from friends, relatives, or your lawyer or accountant. You can also use the Internet as a resource for finding a reputable agent. Connect with thousands of members of the National Association of Insurance and Financial Advisors (NAIFA) on **www.life-line.org/find_agent.html**.

- The agent you choose should come from a reputable firm that has a good financial rating. He or she should also have expertise in the field, which can be determined by professional designations like CLU or CFP.

- He or she turns difficult financial lingo into easily understood terms. The person you choose should also understand your financial and personal situations, as well as the risks you are comfortable with and willing to take.

- Your insurance agent should draw up a personalized recommendation as to specific features of different plans and why they work for you. He or she should not pressure you into a decision; rather, the right agent will work with you and let you decide which policy best suits your needs.

Financial Advisers

If you need to change or reinvest the deceased person's financial holdings, you can find help from financial advisers, banks, or trust companies as long as you take these actions in the best interest of the beneficiaries. A financial adviser can help you take advantage of safe opportunities with an investment.

Listen carefully to the advice of financial experts, as you can be held liable if they do not make the proper investments and lose money for the beneficiaries through neglect. This is especially important when you are dealing with a financial adviser in whom the deceased person has placed trust.

If you are in the position of selecting a financial adviser, you should go about it the same way you would choose any other professional. An adviser should have good credentials, belong to professional organizations or banking centers, and have reputable references.

Choosing the Right Financial Planner

FINANCIAL PLANNER FILES

For most people, it is important to take into consideration with whom they will be working. You need to find someone you can trust — someone you know has your best interests at heart. To do that, ask these questions when searching for a financial planner:

- What is the person/firm's background? What credentials do they have that will fit with what you need and want from them? You want to know this and how it relates to what you need.

- What do they do? One thing that is essential to take note of is the fact that financial planners are all different. It is recommended you choose a Certified Financial Planner® (CFP®), since he or she must pass an exam to become licensed. This follows a long list of financial training courses at the college level. In addition, the financial planner needs to have at least three years of experience working with financial planning clients. While there are many other types of financial planners out there, you want one that has the title to go along with the skills.

- How is the financial planner paid? It is important to determine this about the financial planners you are considering. Those who get a commission from the products that they say you must have are not the best way to go. There is an inherent conflict of interest in such an arrangement. Look for those that are only paid a fee or those that are paid based on how well your portfolio does. Make sure you clearly understand whether or not the financial planner is being paid to sell you a product.

CASE STUDY: TIPS FOR WORKING WITH A FINANCIAL PLANNER

William Russo, CFP
Certified Financial Planner
33595 Bainbridge Road, Suite 104
Solon, Ohio, 44139
Phone: (440) 349-4980
E-mail: Brusso@concordfinancialplan.com
Web site: www.concordfinancialplan.com

The job of the financial planner is to make people take the time to identify their goals, educate them as to the options available, and make sure that their recommendations are followed through. Once a plan is implemented, ongoing review ensures that the plan is modified to take into account changes that occur.

A person should expect to spend an hour to an hour and a half discussing their current situations (net worth, spending plan), goals and priorities, time frames, and what is important to them and why. What got them to this point, what has worked, what has not, what other professionals they work with, and what outcomes they desire to make them feel the relationship is worthwhile are all topics that will be discussed.

My job can only be successful if there is a level of trust and if all information that affects a person's financial affairs is disclosed. This is mutual, as I must be able to convey trust before anyone would feel comfortable disclosing his or her financial affairs, thoughts, and concerns.

A financial planner is a good investment because he or she is an independent entity that can provide objective insight into a person's financial affairs. A planner should never tell a client what they want to hear, but should explain to them the impact of decisions that are made on his or her financial plan. We try to make sure people understand that, to build wealth, they must first spend less than they earn. We see to it that clients commit to and follow a sound, long-term investment strategy. We reinforce the need to stay disciplined and exercise patience.

Accountants

When you need to make business decisions for the estate, accountants can review tax returns, analyze essential operations, and even place a value on those operations. If the deceased person had an accountant, check with him or her and continue the services if they seem satisfactory.

Using a qualified certified public accountant (CPA) is a good way to prepare state and federal estate-tax returns, especially if the estate is complex. As personal representative, you are responsible for estate-tax returns, gift-tax returns, and income taxes. A review of these matters by a knowledgeable accountant is in your best interest, as well as the best interest of the estate and, ultimately, the beneficiaries, who could save thousands of dollars.

Choosing the Right Accountant

ACCOUNTANT FILES

The accountant plays a primary role; therefore, you should have some clear-cut goals when it comes to choosing this advisor for estate planning. Here are some things to look for in a qualified accountant:

- Is he or she a CPA? You want to ensure that the accountant you select is a Certified Public Accountant. This means that he or she has taken the necessary educational steps toward earning a license from the American Institute of Certified Public Accountants, which is not an easy feat.

- Who is the firm? You should ensure that the accountant you hire is not working for anyone that may encourage him or her to sell you products you do not necessarily need. You can easily learn this by simply asking.

- What experience does the accountant have working in estate planning? This is key because many CPAs will have a specialty field; just because they know how to do basic estate planning accounting does not necessarily mean they know all there is to know about it. You want someone that can provide you with a specialty in estate planning.

Professional Appraisers

An expert appraiser is well worth any cost, especially for a sizable estate. Evaluation of family assets, collectibles, or a business requires careful and accurate appraisals for tax reasons and for setting value. The appraiser should be highly professional and have a good track record. Using the U.S. Department of Housing and Urban Development's Web site, you can look up a list of HUD's approved appraisers. Appraisers listed on this site are not guaranteed to be perfect, but they have been approved by this government agency. You can look up HUD-approved appraisers in your area by visiting **https://entp.hud.gov/idapp/ html/apprlook.cfm**.

Business or financial appraisers are uniquely qualified to assess business interests. A careful appraisal of business operations will be helpful for tax reasons and for preparing the business for possible sale — the appraisal provides a correct value for the business and could possibly bring high rewards for beneficiaries.

Collectibles owned by the deceased person may also be highly valued. Specialized appraisers can evaluate stamp and coin collections, antiques, art, and other valuables, including sports memorabilia or doll collections. All of this leads, of course, to the benefit of the heirs.

Real Estate Agents

Amid the housing market's continual ups and downs, real estate agents are an essential part of the estate team. They can help you get the best value on estate property if you must sell it. Discuss the property informally with several agents before choosing one to list the property. The agent should be based in an office that services the area where the property is located and should be specialized in the type of property you are selling, whether it is residential or business.

Even if you are not selling any estate property, keeping in close contact with a real estate agent can help you with any future dealings that may arise with a residential or commercial property. For instance, a rental property owned by the estate may be taking in good income during the probate process, and could become a prized package for beneficiaries as the estate administration nears an end.

Banks or Trust Companies

Financial centers are available to offer services to you as a personal representative, even if the deceased person did not specify a financial institution to turn to for advice. A qualified financial institution can be a strong member of the estate team, providing advice and taking care of financial needs you are not comfortable dealing with on your own.

Banks and trust companies offer assistance in matters such as handling investments from the estate in an account that allows the bank to invest assets in a custodial manner. This is a good alternative if you prefer not to handle investment responsibilities. However, you must remember that you are still responsible for those investments. Because of that, you must choose a reputable bank. Look for banks that offer evidence of their investment performance and an overall portfolio rate earned on common trust funds.

Co-Personal Representatives

You may not be alone as a personal representative. A will may designate a family member as co-representative because of knowledge of the property, or name a bank as co-executor to handle financial matters. Two or more surviving children may be selected.

When an estate does not have a will, courts rarely appoint co-administrators, but it is possible, especially when the estate is complex or when minor children are involved. It is important for co-personal representatives to work together to reach an agreement on major issues. Having co-representatives also relieves you of the burden of handling all estate affairs yourself.

Sometimes, co-personal representatives are chosen because they are family members who understand the personal and financial matters the survivors will face. For instance, siblings might be chosen.

However, because people have the right to renounce the position of personal representative, it is not unusual for one family member to do so. This can happen when the family member lives too far away and prefers that another person in the family handle the details. This would also reduce expenses and perhaps expedite the process.

At other times, co-personal representatives are chosen because each can handle specific areas of the estate. A financial adviser known to the deceased person might be selected to take care of detailed work involving finances or investments. A bank or trust company can also handle this. An attorney known to the family could take care of legal affairs. A son and daughter could take care of the needs of the property or other family members.

Choosing multiple personal representatives can help prevent family conflicts, but it is also an alternative when family members are well-aware they do not have expertise in one area of the estate or another. Either way, this can help speed up the process of dealing with property, assets, and beneficiaries, as well as making sure assets are distributed in the best way.

When co-personal representatives are selected to handle the estate, they must work together for the best interests of the beneficiaries and in accordance with the deceased person's wishes. They should be in agreement with each other about estate matters.

When you create a will, it is essential to be aware of this and choose the right people to work as a team. If you see possible conflict among co-executors, you should make provisions for this in the will. For example, you could give one co-executor precedence over another in the case of any disagreements.

Regardless, the people chosen as co-personal representatives should work as hard as possible to reach an agreement on issues. They are responsible for estate matters, so it only makes sense for them to consult with each other and keep each other advised on various issues, especially if one person has more expertise than another in a particular area.

Guardians

A deceased person might choose a guardian to take personal care of his or her children. This also can be done by court appointment when a minor is involved, or a surviving parent can select a guardian if the parent for some reason is unable to live with the child.

As personal representative of the estate, you must make certain that the needs of minor beneficiaries are being met and that funds from the estate are being used properly for the children. You may have to make sure social security, veterans', or employee benefits have been applied for and are being disbursed properly, or that necessary educational and medical assistance is being handled. The guardian may be there to take care of the child's daily needs, but it is your job to watch over the present and future benefits owed to the beneficiary, who usually stays under guardianship until reaching the age of maturity.

The deceased person might also select a guardian for property if beneficiaries cannot handle it because of age or other reasons, perhaps because a surviving relative is not mentally or physically able to oversee it. It is your job to turn over to the guardian of the property the assets to which the beneficiaries are entitled.

The Family of the Deceased Person

Meeting with the family is, of course, essential at the start of estate administration to review the terms of the will or trust, explain the functions of the attorney and personal representative, describe the steps that need to be taken, and obtain information from the family. It is also important to meet with the heirs on a regular basis to keep them informed during the process. Family members can always offer information that might help in any legal or financial affairs. They may have once thought this information private or unnecessary, but it might now provide insight for resolving an issue.

Lack of communication with beneficiaries is often a reason why personal representatives are sued. A good personal representative or trustee keeps a solid relationship with the beneficiaries and communicates on a regular basis. You may even develop a friendship to avoid any conflict that may have occurred otherwise. Frequent communication also resolves issues that might be causing delays in transferring assets to beneficiaries. If you cannot keep in touch in person, make contact regularly by phone or e-mail. This type of contact can even be a necessity when you have a short amount of time to make an estate decision. You are still keeping the beneficiary apprised of the situation, and he or she may even volunteer input that could be of assistance.

In any case, you must consider the deceased person's family a part of the estate team, especially if they are beneficiaries concerned about your actions in administering the estate.

CHAPTER 6

Preparing for a Death

As difficult as it is to face the death of a close friend or relative who is suffering from a lingering or terminal illness, it is also the best opportunity to get everything in order while you can. This is in the best interest of the dying person, the beneficiaries, and the personal representative. It is a difficult task, but it will make the process easier when death comes.

This is a time to think about and prepare for administration of the estate, increase the estate's size (if possible) to help beneficiaries, reduce costs wherever possible, take measures to decrease income tax, provide cash to pay tax and other expenses, and defer payment of taxes. Doing this before the actual administration of the estate will lift a tremendous burden from the personal representative's shoulders, and it will make the actual transition of the estate and assets easier and more fairly balanced. It could save an enormous amount of time and be financially beneficial to everyone involved.

Power of Attorney, Important Documents

When a dying relative or friend appoints you as personal representative, you might want to have the person sign a durable power of attorney, which gives you or someone else the right to act on behalf of the dying person. Durable means you can use the power to take actions if the dying person becomes incapacitated, much like the authorization used in a revocable living trust. It also allows someone who is not a licensed lawyer to handle legal matters, such as signing tax returns and taking important tax-saving measures.

Power of Attorneys: An Overview

There are three main categories under which a power of attorney may fall. Each of these types of POA will be discussed in detail in later chapters.

- **Health care**: A durable health care POA can cover many medical decisions that need to be made on your behalf should you become unable to give consent for a procedure to take place.

- **Childcare**: A childcare POA allows for some medical decisions to be made on behalf of your child if he or she is not living with you for whatever reason.

- **Financial**: A financial POA allows for someone to make business decisions, purchases, or other decisions or deals with your money on your behalf if you are not present.

Document Title	Purpose	Notes
General Power of Attorney	Specifies certain areas of financial affairs to be managed by an attorney-in-fact.	Effective immediately. Invalid upon your divorce, death, revocation, or incapacity.
Unlimited Power of Attorney	Assigns all areas of your financial affairs to an attorney-in-fact.	Effective immediately. Invalid upon your divorce, death, revocation, or incapacity.
Limited Power of Attorney	Specifies certain areas of your financial affairs, or certain transactions or prevailing conditions, or certain periods in which an attorney-in-fact is authorized to represent you.	Invalid upon your divorce, death, revocation, or incapacity.
Power of Attorney for Real Estate	Designates a representative to act in your place for the purpose of transferring a particular piece of property.	Invalid upon your divorce, death, revocation, or incapacity.
Power of Attorney for Childcare	Designates a representative to act in your place as parent or guardian for the purpose of childcare in temporary situations.	Invalid upon your divorce, death, revocation, or incapacity.
Durable Financial Power of Attorney	Assigns responsibilities for your financial affairs to an attorney-in-fact, to be effective either continuously (despite your incapacity) or to become effective (upon your incapacity).	Effective as specified in the document and remains in effect until your revocation or death.
Durable Power of Attorney for Health Care	Names a chosen representative to serve as advocate for your interests in the event you become unable to make decisions because of medical reasons.	Effective upon your incapacity and remains in effect for the duration of your life, until your revocation, until you regain mental capacity, or death.

Finding and saving important documents

Locate and list bank accounts; life, health, fire, liability, and other insurance policies; real estate deeds; wills and trusts; stocks; bonds; other securities; birth certificates; marriage licenses; marital agreements; military service records; and social security information. You should list names, addresses, and phone numbers of family members and key advisers and place them in a secure deposit box or other safe place. Review and change the documents whenever necessary to update them.

Ask the dying person if he or she chooses to sign a living will, which can be used or not used to prolong life by extraordinary means. This makes it easier on doctors and family members to honor such wishes. This might also be the right time to ask the person if he or she is interested in anatomical gifts for organ donation or medical research. If so, the person can sign the appropriate forms, which you can later give to the appropriate people or hospitals. If the person is strongly against anatomical gifts, he or she should state this in a will or letter of instructions. This will make it easier on family members and medical personnel. With a letter of instructions, the dying person can let immediate relatives and friends know of his or her wishes regarding personal matters that might need to be taken care of immediately after death. These instructions can also advise people close to the dying person about financial, legal, and final wishes.

Adding Value to the Estate

Increase the size of the estate and the amounts that will go to heirs by exploring possibilities for extended term insurance. You may be able to convert a life insurance policy into a term policy.

This relieves the financial burden of premium payments, while continuing the full amount of coverage for a limited time period. Or, check for waiver-of-premium clauses that require the insurance company to continue the policy in full force in the event of disability. Decrease income taxes by looking for immediate charitable gifts, and make donations before the person's death.

In 2010, each person in a family can give each recipient up to $13,000 free of gift taxes. This takes money away from the estate so it cannot be taxed, while also making sure money goes to the intended beneficiaries.

Life insurance is usually not subject to legal fees and other transfer actions. Most states leave life insurance free from taxes. Make sure the policy does not name the estate as its beneficiary because this could make the proceeds subject to credit claims and state inheritance taxes.

Avoiding Probate and Other Actions to Take

When a person is dying from a terminal illness, he or she may still have time to save loved ones the expensive and time-consuming procedure of probate by restructuring property ownership. This can reduce the possibility of conflict among family members when the time comes. If minor children and the other parent are not involved, which usually calls for probate, the dying person can look at a few options.

Ask the person about setting up a revocable trust, which he or she can alter, amend, or terminate at any time before death. This trust will provide for property management before and after death. It will also avoid costs and delays brought on by the probate process. The dying person owns the property in a sense (as a trustee), but the person or persons named as successors automatically become the legal owner upon death.

If a property is not already in joint tenancy, it might be time to consider taking such a measure for the title to pass automatically to the surviving joint tenant, avoiding probate. It is quite common for spouses to have joint tenancy, but this setup has drawbacks. For instance, if both spouses die in the same accident, the property would have to be probated because there is no surviving owner. Joint ownership with a spouse also has negative income-tax consequences to consider.

Other people can share property because there is no limit to the number of persons who can own property as joint tenants. It is possible to add children as joint tenants in case anything happens to both parents, and the children will receive the property automatically upon the parents' death. However, adding children as joint tenants would be considered a gift. This could generate a gift tax, depending on the property's value.

While the dying person is living, he or she can complete certain tasks to avoid time-consuming actions and frustration after death. For example, if the person owns a business, he or she can take the necessary steps to sell it, pass it on to someone else, or complete the necessary agreements with a partner. The person can also arrange for the business to pay estate taxes. Some businesses can exclude more than $1 million from the estate. Check with a qualified attorney about these exclusions.

If the person has property in more than one state, he or she should take the time to establish a permanent residence to avoid estate and property taxation by two or more states. The person should live in the house of the desired state for more than one year. Also, the person should register to vote, transfer all bank accounts, change addresses for credit cards and social security checks, apply for a driver's license, and file tax returns in that state.

Leaving property to a surviving spouse makes it possible to eliminate all federal estate taxes when transferring the property. Check to see if the dying person wants to do this.

CHAPTER 7

Preparations After Death

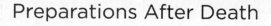

Whether or not the deceased person was able to make pre-death estate preparations, you will need to deal with certain matters as soon as possible after his or her death to continue the smooth transition of property.

Immediate Concerns

Close family members or friends often make the funeral and burial arrangements before they know about the appointment of a personal representative. Even so, they should follow any directions that might be listed in a will or letter of instructions as closely as possible. Immediate family members should use this time to locate any instructions left in a will, or learn whether the deceased person spoke to anyone about making anatomical donations. If this is the case, the family should immediately contact the appropriate hospital or medical school. Obviously, many organs need to be transplanted within hours of a person's death.

Even though the immediate family handles quickly-arranged funeral and burial procedures, the personal representative receives the bill and pays all costs using the estate's assets. No matter what the cost, the funeral and burial arrangements are made in accordance with the wishes of the family members, unless the deceased person's wishes are immediately known. Funerals can be extremely costly, and whether it is an expected or unexpected death, decisions are made rapidly. This is one of the major reasons people sign pre-burial agreements, taking a heavy burden off the shoulders of the surviving family members. Funerals also often depend on the deceased person's religious beliefs and practices, so certain rituals may need to be followed.

This is an extremely emotional time for close family members, and decisions about funerals and burial — if not pre-arranged — can be unreasonable and lead to high expenses that are often unnecessary. Depend on a reputable funeral director to handle the situation with care and understanding, and to provide the survivors with a wide range of offers, none of them undignified. A reputable funeral home will follow The Funeral Rule set forth by the Federal Trade Commission (FTC), meaning that they should provide all fees out in the open, hiding nothing. Even with a variety of options, the costs of funerals are extremely high. Pre-arrangements can lessen the expense. If the family does not know about any arrangements, it is their first responsibility to locate any document that might provide instructions. Even if it does not keep costs down, it at least adheres to the deceased person's wishes.

The same goes for a burial plot. The family should try to locate a cemetery deed immediately. Often, families make previous arrangements for a burial plot even if they have not made burial pre-arrangements. The funeral director and nearby cemeteries can help you with this. A burial plot purchased before death keeps costs down, the same as pre-death funeral arrangements, while also relieving the emotional burden family members must face.

If your appointment as personal representative is known before the funeral, it is your duty to make sure arrangements are made according to the instructions left in the deceased person's will. Although the will is formally read following the funeral, anyone appointing a personal representative needs to tell that person before death about any funeral arrangements, as well as inform family members. He or she should also communicate instructions for organ donations, place of burial, and any preference for funeral services.

Gathering information can be difficult and complicated if the deceased person lived alone with no professional contacts, family members, or close friends. As the personal representative, you should contact close relatives, local probate offices, and other courts that will inform you about the correct procedures under state and county regulations.

You can always seek advice from the family. If immediate expenses arise following the death, close relatives may know about life insurance policies, which can quickly take care of all funeral costs, as well as other expenses facing the estate. If the deceased person did not leave a will, you must use knowledge gained from communicating with relatives, friends, or other members of the estate team.

A Valid Will

There are, of course, different requirements concerning valid wills among the states. Just because you find a will does not necessarily mean it is valid. If you find a will, immediately show it to an attorney.

Family members may be uncertain about whether the deceased person left a will. They should immediately look around the deceased person's home and in safe-deposit boxes. However, make sure a family member or estate attorney is present when opening the box so that its contents can be verified and so nothing is removed improperly. Some financial institutions even require an employee to be there when the box is opened. This is a good time to present the death certificate to the bank, which will probably allow you to remove the will from the safe-deposit box. If you do find a safe-deposit box, make an inventory of the contents. Life insurance policies, stocks, bonds, and other important assets could be there.

You may find a will in areas of the home where the deceased person kept other important documents, such as an office file or a firesafe. Checking with a family member or close friend may provide a clue. Wills are also kept with attorneys, banks, business associates, or even close friends. Turn the will over to an attorney as soon as possible for probate court filing.

It is important to find a will as soon as possible, if there is one. Even though a will can be considered valid in many states long after the deceased person's death, you would have to make readjustments in order to apply it. The result could turn into a nightmare for families and beneficiaries, especially if they have already addressed many property issues.

If you find something that expresses the deceased person's final wishes, but does not appear to be a legal document, do not assume it is not a legitimate will. Although there have been many cases of phony wills being presented before the court and causing delays and exorbitant legal fees, many states accept handwritten notes on pieces of paper as valid wills after they are carefully examined. Have legal experts look at any notes that appear to be wills or copies of wills. The court will accept them as valid if they turn out to be the legitimate last desires of the deceased person.

Preparing the Will for Probate

After a valid will is produced and given to an attorney to be filed with the probate court, and after all other immediate concerns are taken care of, review the will to learn how the deceased person wanted you to handle the estate as personal representative.

This is the best time to prepare to act in accordance with the deceased person's intentions. The will may make certain statements about family members, businesses, or investments. You must let the provisions of the will guide you, making sure property and assets go to the right people. Sometimes, a will may not be specific, or the deceased person's intentions are not fully clear. You would then have to seek legal advice for certain issues. Ultimately, the probate court may have to resolve ambiguities in the will unless all heirs and beneficiaries agree. In any case, you should have a basic understanding of what the deceased person wanted in order to proceed.

Regardless of how well a will is prepared, it is still possible someone will contest it. Most of the time, this will be a family member, business associate, or other person who has not received what he or she expected as an inheritance. The contesting person may make claims that the deceased person was not in his or her right mind when drawing up the will, was pressured by someone, or was the victim of fraud. The contesting person hopes to use these grounds to have the court invalidate the will. During these legal proceedings, no matter how bitter, it is your job as personal representative to continue with the normal activities of handling the estate while the court decides the merits of the case.

Wills 101

The following sections describe the different type of wills you might encounter as you sort through the particulars of the estate.

Simple wills

A simple will is the most common type of will today. These wills are not joint wills, as they serve only for one person. In addition, they are a single piece of documentation that describes your wishes. When this type of will is used, it will state that the document belongs to a specific person. It will list the beneficiaries, including any charities, and their addresses and birth dates. In addition, it will name the executor of the will and, possibly, a secondary executor in case the first cannot take on the responsibility. It will also include directions for who will care for the person's children and property, as well as distribute assets as the person directs.

Handwritten wills

You may have heard of the term "holographic will." This is a completely handwritten will signed only by the testator without witnesses. Only a few states recognize this type of will, and usually only in certain cases.

Joint wills

A joint will is a type of will that two people, usually a husband and wife, write together as one document. This is not a common practice because the will becomes not only a last will and testament, but also a contract between the two people who have made it. Normally, if a will is made, the person has the right to change it or add to it, or completely revoke it in favor of a new one. If a joint will is made with another, he or she may be giving up his or her rights to revoke the will.

Mutual wills

Another type of will that you may be able to use is a mutual will. In this type of will, two people can have their wills or estate plans linked together. The legalities of this type of will are important to understand, so ensure that you work with an attorney that knows the ins and outs of mutual wills.

Other types of wills

Although the wills discussed previously are rarely used — except for the simple will — the following wills are additional options that can be even more limiting. Most states have strict laws on these types of wills that you must know about before you attempt to use them.

- *Nuncupative:* This will, also known as an oral will, is one that is spoken. The only time that this will can be used, in most cases, is when someone is on his or her deathbed. If you are going to die within minutes, this type of will can be used in highly unusual circumstances.

- *Electronic wills:* Another type of will that has been seen appearing is the electronic will. Only Nevada allows this type of will, though. If a Nevada resident has created a will in electronic format, such as on the computer, this could be an option, but it is not that easy. In addition to the actual electronic recording, there must be a way of identifying who wrote the will, which could include fingerprints, retinal scans, or voice recognition. Sometimes, it is required to have a specialized program to write the will that will include an electronic signature.

- *Video wills:* You see these all the time on television, but no state allows a will to be video recorded as the sole way of communicating your wishes. You can recite your wishes over video and communicate your needs through video, but only if you also have a legal document in place. This is a good addition to your legal will, however, especially when you believe that the will might be contested.

CHAPTER 8

Probate

Probate is a process to prove the validity of the will, or a process for a personal representative to handle the affairs of the estate. Property left by the deceased person is subject to probate and may require court supervision unless the property is in a trust, in which case it is not registered in the deceased person's own name. Property subject to probate includes real estate, stocks and bonds, bank accounts, and other assets owned under an individual's name. Written contracts stipulated to go to beneficiaries are exempt, including life insurance policies, profit sharing, 401(k) plans, and individual retirement accounts (IRAs). Jointly owned property is passed automatically to the surviving owner. A will controls the property owned by the deceased person for the disposition of assets, but is still subject to probate. Some states may not require probate court if the property does not exceed a specific dollar amount, and you may be able to handle the legalities of these cases through the clerk of the probate court without an attorney.

Probate Process

Probate is usually handled in the state and county where the deceased person lived at the time of death. Personal property and real estate is subject to probate. The time it takes for probate to be completed depends on the size of the estate. It can take from a few months to a few years, or can even drag on for decades when objections to the will arise.

State law or county regulations sometimes set the cost of probate. This can include appraisal costs, personal representative fees, court costs, legal fees, and accounting fees. The total cost can range from 3 to 7 percent of the estate's total value. When the will is contested and the process becomes long, however, the costs can be far more expensive.

Depending on the state, some estates are exempt from probate if they are valued below a certain amount. A title to a property that is jointly owned may be transferred under the right of survivorship. If the only assets are insurance, retirement funds, or employee benefits, they can be transferred without probate. Some states even allow certain real estate properties to pass on to the beneficiaries automatically. Consult a qualified attorney to find out whether the estate needs to be probated.

Even if probate is necessary, many states outline simplified procedures for particular circumstances. Probate may still be a good idea if there are credit claims against the estate and it needs to go through the regular legal process to avoid complicated conditions in the future, including lawsuits.

Some people think a small estate does not need the added complication of going through probate, especially if the deceased person left a valid will. The purpose of probate, however, is for the court to validate the will and handle any potential contests before it becomes official. For instance, the court can rule a will invalid if evidence shows that a later will was drawn up, that the deceased was not mentally competent when signing the will, or that fraud or forgery was involved.

You or the estate attorney will go through several easy procedures, starting with a visit to the county court that handles the probate of wills. The office may have different names, depending on the state or county, but inquiring about where to find the "probate office" will help you locate it. You will then present the clerk with an official death certificate for the deceased person, as well as a petition to present the will to probate (prepared by you or the attorney beforehand) for review, approval, and signatures.

You will also present an original will if the deceased person had one. Copies are not accepted. Witnesses to the will should be there with you, if possible, to save time or any delays. Many states, however, have self-proving wills that all parties sign so that witnesses do not have to appear.

The court then reviews and verifies all the information you presented. When the probate office is satisfied with the information, it will name you the will's executor and give you letters testamentary. If there is no will, the court will appoint an administrator or equivalent personal representative and issue letters of administration, which authorize him or her to act on behalf of the estate.

You will frequently need copies of these letters when dealing with estate issues. You will present them to banks, other financial institutions, creditors, debtors, beneficiaries, heirs, accountants, the funeral director, and attorneys — to name a few instances of use.

During the probate process, it is your job as personal representative to:

- Determine whether there are any probate assets, and then identify and gather those assets.

- Value and appraise the assets.

- Receive payments owed to the estate, including interest, dividends, and other income, such as unpaid salary, vacation pay, and other company benefits. Give legal notice to potential creditors and investigate the validity of all claims against the estate.

- Set up a checking account for the estate; pay funeral bills and outstanding debts.

- Pay expenses of the estate, as well as the day-to-day functions of the estate, including filing and paying income and estate taxes.

- Distribute property in accordance with the will and close probate.

Failure to perform these duties can result in legal action. You may have to pay out of your own pocket for losses brought to the estate.

CASE STUDY: GETTING THROUGH PROBATE

Law Offices of James N. Reyer, P.A.
5301 North Federal Highway, Suite 130
Boca Raton, FL 33487
(561) 241-9003 - voice
(561) 988-9892 - fax

Probate is the process through which a person's assets pass to his or her beneficiaries at the time of death through the oversight and supervision of a court. The assets in a probate matter are those that a person held in his or her name alone, and that do not automatically pass to the beneficiaries.

The court proceeding ensures that all assets are properly administered, that all beneficiaries receive their appropriate shares of the estate, and that all estate creditors are paid. A court will supervise the terms and conditions of the deceased person's last will and testament or, in the absence of a will, the statutory terms for the passing on of property at death. Probate can be a simple procedure in some states and a complex one in others. The complexity of probate is also determined by the size of the estate, the number and type of assets, creditor claims, and the cooperation (or lack thereof) of the beneficiaries.

The best manner in which to handle probate is to hire competent legal representation to see you and the beneficiaries through the process. This is mandated by statute in some states, but it is always a sound practice. The most important thing to do during the administration of an estate is to properly identify the assets in the estate, clarify ownership, and disclose to all beneficiaries exactly how the process will transpire and when to expect a distribution.

Probate is not always necessary. Proper estate-planning techniques can pass probate altogether through vehicles such as a revocable living trust or a life estate deed. In addition, if multiple people own assets (for example, a "joint tenancy with the right of survivorship" designation) upon the death of one owner, the surviving owner or owners will acquire title to the asset without the need for a legal process.

When a person dies without a will, the state he or she lives in has a will drawn up for him or her. This is legally called "intestacy." It is a common fallacy that, when someone dies without a will, his or her assets pass to the state. This is not true. Every state has a statutory schedule of who inherits property if a person dies without a will. This results in close relatives taking ownership of the assets. Sometimes, this is not what the deceased person would have wished. Draft your estate-planning documents to reflect what you want, so that your beneficiaries will not have to rely on statutes. Close family members can, to some extent, modify the statutory distribution if they are entitled to shares and do not want to take them. Put your wishes on paper as prepared by a competent estate-planning attorney.

Select and Meet the Attorney

Do you always need a lawyer when handling probate? The answer may be no if you are administering a simple estate without conflicts and if it is easy to understand what is being transferred. It is always wise, however, to at least consult with an attorney knowledgeable in estate matters. Many formalities are necessary before the probate court, and one simple mistake could end up costing you a fortune in fees and time wasted.

Most estate experts will advise you to use an attorney for the probate process. A qualified lawyer will not only guide you through the process, but also might discover a legal matter that will save or earn you thousands of dollars. New laws regarding insurance or estate matters are introduced frequently into state legislation. Only a qualified attorney might know about them. The bottom line is that if you do not know what you are doing, get a lawyer. You will sleep easier and might even be rewarded with more time and money.

The deceased person may have recommended an attorney in the will, as mentioned in Chapter 5, but you are not bound by that; you, as personal representative, are now accountable for all matters regarding the estate. The attorney the deceased person suggested might be the best one for the job in many cases if he or she handled many of the deceased person's affairs and is a longtime associate or friend. Sometimes, however, the relationship could have formed years ago and the attorney is no longer familiar with the deceased person's latest ventures. Or, the attorney may no longer have an interest in this type of work or even be qualified to do it.

If you think you need an attorney, check with the local bar association or in the yellow pages for estate-planning attorneys. Bankers, accountants, and other lawyers not in that particular field might also refer you to a knowledgeable attorney. Ask family members, too. Just be sure they are not recommending a friend or favorite relative, unless that attorney proves to be highly qualified. Family members can be a good source of information, especially if they are knowledgeable about credible attorneys in the area, but do your homework just as you would when investigating on your own. Depending on the size and complexity of the estate, the attorney will be working as hard as, or more than, you will during the probate process. Select the attorney carefully, keeping in mind that he or she will be a member of the estate team.

Like the personal representative, the lawyer should be impartial, with no conflicts of interest regarding the deceased person or property. The attorney informs the representative or trustee of the tasks involved in administering the estate and is responsible for drafting all legal documents to present before the probate court. The attorney will tell you about documents and information that you must gather in settling the estate. If certain tasks are too much for you to handle, you may need to hire an accountant, financial adviser, appraiser, or real estate agent.

Once you have chosen an attorney, you will have an initial meeting to discuss the will and/or trust and the duties and responsibilities of the personal representative and the attorney. You also may be discussing other estate-related issues, such as giving allowances to surviving family members, as well as the initial steps you need to take for administration. The level of consultation depends on your knowledge in this legal area.

Can Probate Be a Good Thing?

There are some times when probate can be a good thing, such as when an estate has a large amount of debt. Often, this is the best way for money owed to be settled.

If there are debts that exceed what would be considered normal, everyday household costs, you may not want to avoid probate.

Those who only have:

- Mortgages;

- Car or other vehicle payments;

- Credit card debt;

- Small debts such as subscriptions;

or

- Utility bills

...do not want to file probate.

Those who have:

- Debts that are larger from a business;

- A failed business;

- Large amounts owed to creditors that they know will come after their home;

or

- Pending lawsuits or claims against them

...do want to file probate, especially if you, as the executor, plan to fight those claims. Here, probate can help resolve creditor liability and can handle the legal action that many creditors will use to try to get their slice of the estate pie.

Initial Steps

As personal representative, you should obtain important documents as soon as possible, including the deceased person's social security number, home address, date of birth and date of death; birth dates for all minor children; names, addresses, phone numbers, and relationships of all beneficiaries named in the will or heirs by law if there was no will; names and addresses of all witnesses to the will; a preliminary list of assets subject to probate, and nonprobate assets; a preliminary list of known debts of the deceased person; copies of deeds, leases, contracts, and trusts; copies of pension, profit sharing, 401(k), IRA and other employee-benefit-plan documents; and three years of income-tax returns.

Other initial steps would include hiring professionals for the estate team and outlining key due dates, including court hearings, filings, and tax-return deadlines.

Another important step will be meeting with the family or beneficiaries. They are the logical sources for information about the documents you need and possibly heirs you need to locate and contact.

Conduct a meeting with the family along with the estate attorney and the trustee, if that person is someone other than you. Review the terms of the will and trust. Explain the functions of the personal representative, attorney, and trustee. Describe the steps that need to be taken to settle the estate. Outline a timetable and gather information.

Personal representatives and trustees are in charge of a deceased person's affairs until completion of the administration of the estate. During a meeting with the family, a personal representative and attorney should explain all legal rights heirs have regarding the estate. This may be a time to discuss any immediate financial needs for the beneficiaries and the possible funds that are available. It is important that you provide financial support for the beneficiaries, if needed, during administration of the estate. If you are a close friend or relative of the deceased person, you may already be familiar with their situations. Otherwise, a first meeting is a good time to find out.

Other Probate Factors

If the deceased person did not have a will, intestacy law of the state takes over and governs the distribution of assets. Some states may provide a certain amount to a surviving spouse. Some states may divide the assets equally among surviving children. In other cases, deceased persons have chosen not to draw up a will because they were in uncomplicated situations in which assets could be passed on with no problem.

When you will not need an attorney

You may not need to retain an attorney for the transition of assets if it is determined that the estate's assets can be passed over to the beneficiaries without the need for probate court. It also could be possible that your duties for the estate will be so routine and minor that you can accomplish them easily. Most attorneys provide a free consultation for you to find out whether probate is indeed necessary.

The right location

The deceased person's permanent home may sometimes make the difference in the cost of probate. Say you are getting ready to retire and have homes in two different states. For the best interests of your future estate, you might choose for your permanent residence the state that has more liberal tax laws than the other.

CHAPTER 9

Administering the Estate

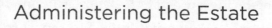

Secure the deceased person's residence by protecting personal items, changing the person's mailing address to yours, getting authority over bank and brokerage accounts, and making sure property and valuable assets are properly insured. Bank accounts, stocks and bonds, mutual funds, real estate, life insurance, mortgages, and notes are assets that should be valued as of the date of the deceased person's death. The estate may face tax penalties if assets are undervalued. If the deceased person had a business, that will also be part of administering the estate.

How to Handle Funds

Determining how much money you need to cover estate taxes should be a priority that you deal with as soon as possible. The deceased person's will or local law determines whether the personal representative is authorized to sell estate assets to pay expenses or meet other cash needs. You must handle debts incurred prior to death as claims against the estate. You also must submit notice of death to creditors. If a creditor files a previously unknown claim after the notice has expired, it is not valid. As personal representative, you are entitled to certain fees for service, and the probate court usually handles these fees.

Setting up a checking or savings account is another top priority when administering an estate because it is one of your best tools in record-keeping. You are required to report to local, state, and federal taxing authorities, the beneficiaries, and the courts whenever a formal accounting is necessary. This includes money and other property that goes to creditors, agents, employees, and various authorities.

A checking account functions as a central financial funnel and establishes a strong record that banks can verify because it shows exactly how much money has gone out and how much is received. Personal representatives should keep just enough money in the account to meet regular bills as they are due. Some banks establish a special account for estates that can make it easier for you to administer cash flows and payments.

Meet with several banks to determine the type and cost of accounts, as well as the services they offer. Using the same bank used by the deceased person is often advisable. Or, you could use a bank you have done business with in the past. The estate's attorney also can make suggestions in selecting the best bank for the estate.

Proper record-keeping means keeping track of each financial transaction involving the estate and describing the background of each deposit, as well as getting details of dividends and stocks sold. Itemize other details to make sure you have an accurate account of the estate's finances. Keep separate records to track the history of each asset. Use separate files with documentation for bills and other expenses, including receipts for sales of stocks or securities to show profits or losses.

Safe-deposit boxes can be a source of valuable information about the deceased person. They might contain various receipts, deeds, mortgages, insurance policies, stock certificates, and personal papers. Jewelry and other valuables, including cash, also can be held in a safe-deposit box.

Family members most likely would be aware of a safe-deposit box, as would banks and businesses the deceased person dealt with.

State laws on access to safe-deposit boxes vary. Some states permit a surviving spouse to open the box if it is held in both their names. Companies the deceased person served as a corporate officer would be able to access the box if it is held in the company's name.

Other states require the bank to seal the box on the date of the deceased person's death, and allow access only in the presence of state or local government officials. This is to prevent possible tax evasion or accumulation of unreported money by the deceased person.

You can open a safe-deposit box with representatives present if you think a will, deeds, or insurance policies to pay for funeral expenses could be available. In some states, you must schedule an appointment with the bank to gain access to the deposit box, as local, state, and corporate representatives may need to be there.

An attorney can advise you on the details involved in opening safe-deposit boxes, depending on each situation. Some family members inadvertently violate state laws by getting into the box before the bank or other authorities are aware of the death. For example, a person might retrieve materials from a deposit box the day after a relative dies, while the funeral home and local authorities are still processing information on the death. Bank representatives may not be aware of the death when the person comes in to open the box. This, however, could result in criminal prosecution of that person. Consulting with an attorney or bank official will help personal representatives and heirs know ahead of time how to handle safe-deposit boxes.

As personal representative, you need to be fully aware of all matters handled by the deceased person. You can notify the post office and have the deceased person's mail sent to you so you learn about any business dealings, debts, and bills owed to the person. Contact businesses you know the deceased person was involved with, as well as creditors and debtors.

You or the estate attorney will notify creditors and debtors of a person's death through newspaper advertisements and other methods. The reason for this is to make sure that everyone who had contact with the deceased person is notified of the death and can deal with any debts or credits.

Your state may have laws that stipulate when and where you should place these advertisements. Again, an attorney can be helpful at this time. In many states, you are not permitted to end your duties as personal representative until these advertisements have been properly placed, so that all businesses, creditors, and debtors have had sufficient time to learn of the death. This is important to beneficiaries who cannot receive their shares of the estate until you complete this action. Creditors have a specified period of time to respond to the notices of death, and the statute of limitations can run from several months to a year. The notices can also alert long-lost relatives to the person's death.

Preparing Inventory

Before starting a detailed inventory of the deceased person's assets, you should first determine whether he or she had any outstanding credit claims at death. Sometimes, you can turn these claims into cash for the estate or the beneficiaries. For instance, if the deceased person owned a business and was owed money by a customer on credit, that customer would still owe the money to the business, which means it would be considered an asset for the estate. Find loans and other assets owed to the deceased person by looking through the person's records or checking with family members of associates. Owed bills, such as a tenant leaving an apartment with rent still due or other claims that may require civil action, would be difficult to find.

As personal representative, you must know as much as possible about the deceased person's business and other dealings that require record-keeping and accounting. This means reviewing all books and records, and then making a list of potential claims using the documentation available to you. Supporting documentation will bolster your position if a family member or beneficiary questions an asset of the estate. This is also a time to seek the advice of professionals, such as attorneys or accountants, who are familiar with these measures.

An inventory of the estate's assets is not always necessary for the probate court, but is almost always a good idea in your job as personal representative. It will keep your records accurate and up-to-date in case any legal questions arise later. You should make a draft inventory first to find out the most important assets, and then make a formal inventory.

Find out which assets belong to the estate by checking with an attorney or another estate or finance professional. Some assets may automatically go to a surviving spouse, as in jointly owned property.

As you make an inventory of the assets, decisions on the deceased person's investments or business operations most likely will become a priority. Make sure you reinvest assets properly so the estate does not suffer any future losses. Be aware of the specifics of each asset to know which ones you should deal with first, saving you and the beneficiaries time and money at the completion of estate administration.

Tangible and Intangible Property

Tangible personal property includes actual items you can touch, such as jewelry, furniture, or automobiles Intangible items include stock certificates, insurance policies, and other nonphysical materials that are redeemed for monetary value.

It is not your job to make a profit for the estate or the beneficiaries. For instance, you should sell a stock only if, according to a qualified financial adviser, it looks like the stock will lose money and you would be helping the beneficiaries by preventing a loss. This, of course, is not always an easy issue to deal with because even experts can be wrong or unsure of a financial investment's value. Make a careful analysis before reaching a conclusion about the sale or reinvestment of a stock. In some situations, the decision can be obvious, especially if several investment advisers agree which direction a stock is headed in the financial market. At other times, the best advisers in the market can have different opinions. Regardless, your decisions always need to be in the best interest of the estate and the beneficiaries.

Business operations are similar to investments in that you, as personal representative, can be held liable for any losses the business suffers. Follow the instructions of the will, or use your best judgment if there is no will, when deciding whether to sell a business or retain it for the estate. You also bear the responsibility of keeping the business in good shape before you sell it or pass it over to a partner. If you do not have expertise in operating a particular venture, hire a professional manager who can handle it in the meantime. Keep the business profitable and in good hands until you sell it, or until your job as personal representative is complete.

Make the same careful analysis when dealing with real estate, whether commercial or residential. You might have to collect income from rents or sales, and you should invest the proceeds in an interest-bearing checking or savings account that keeps the estate in financial good standing. You can also use this income to pay expenses and other cash needs for the estate, depending on the deceased person's wishes and state or local law.

Keep track of all cash requirements for the estate and identify assets that you need to liquidate or deem appropriate for sale. During this process, keep in close contact with the beneficiaries — they might find a particular asset of value or may want you to use it as a financial advance for funds the estate needs.

Get a professional appraisal for tangible property before selling or distributing it. Household furnishings that have no particular value are easy to assess, but items such as art, collectibles, and antiques require appraisal by a knowledgeable professional.

Automobiles are treated like all other possessions belonging to the estate except when jointly owned. In that case, the car would go to a spouse or other partner through the right of survivorship. Even so, when transferring the title or selling the vehicle, check with the rules and regulations of the local Department of Motor Vehicles.

Of course, you should distribute any piece of property to a beneficiary whom the deceased person specifically mentioned in the will or in written instructions. If you decide that you must sell tangible property, take steps to sell it as soon as possible. You do not want the property to lose value and suffer a loss for the estate and the beneficiaries. Give written notice to the beneficiaries of any potential sale of assets. The beneficiaries then have an opportunity to buy the property at a fair market value. Reviewing sale plans with the beneficiaries also helps you avoid conflict among them. You may decide to donate some property to charity, such as furniture or other household items, which would provide valuable income-tax deductions for the estate. To avoid possible conflicts of interest, do not purchase tangible assets for yourself.

CHAPTER 10

Tax Considerations

A s personal representative, you are responsible for filing the final income-tax returns for the deceased person, plus tax returns required for the estate.

Because of tax-relief measures implemented by Congress several years ago, estates are not subject to a federal estate tax in 2010. That is likely to change, though, come 2011. The best advice regarding federal estate taxes is to consult with a tax specialist who will know about the current requirements. This will be important for all aspects of your tax obligations for the estate. For example, many states tie their estate taxes to the federal government's rule. Because of the changing regulations, this is one area not to neglect getting advice on.

Deceased Person's Income-Tax Return

You must file a final personal income-tax return for the deceased person with the IRS within nine months after the date of death, unless you get an extension. You may need to coordinate the filing with a surviving spouse if the deceased person was married at the time of death. The tax return will cover income earned during the year the person died, from January 1 to the date of death.

A helpful guideline in preparing the deceased person's income-tax return will be his or her prior tax returns. If these are not current, you have inherited the job of sorting out that problem as well, as taxes are primary obligations for the estate. Assuming the previous year's tax return is in fair order, it will be a good starting point for you to get a handle on the deceased person's sources of income, deductions, and credits. It is also a valuable source of information for determining the scope of the estate's assets.

Here is a checklist of the main items to consider in putting together necessary information for the deceased person's final federal income-tax return and related tax returns:

- Final paycheck – request W2 from employer

- Income statements from retirement fund sources, if any

- Accrued interest from bank and other financial accounts; obtain accurate statements from each institution and fund

- Business income sources

- Any other sources of income

- Capital gains or losses from sale of property

- Depreciation

- Deductions

- Exemptions

- Charitable contributions

- Tax credits

- Alimony

- Child care

- Medical expenses

- Deductible losses, such as theft or damage

- Self-employment taxes

- Gift tax — gifts exceeding $13,000 (present cap) per individual recipient

- Any other income or tax-relevant information

To some extent, you will be a bit of a financial detective to be sure you obtain all the necessary information. Reasonable due diligence, along with the advice of a tax specialist, should cover what needs to be done. The key is to be thorough, file in a timely manner, pay any tax due, or obtain a refund for the estate if money is due back.

In some cases, a final tax return may not be necessary if the deceased person's income was too little to require it. Since each case has its own unique factors, get all the information about the deceased person's finances before determining whether you will need to file a return.

Estate Taxes

Regardless of whether an estate will ultimately owe taxes, if it has sufficient assets to require probate, you need to obtain a tax identification number for the estate from the IRS. During the time it is open, the estate is considered a distinct entity that receives and distributes assets, pays bills, and reports to the court. As such, it must have its own tax number.

Technically, the federal tax number is called an "employer identification number" (EIN). Although the estate likely will not be an employer, it is considered a legal entity, which theoretically could be an employer. For you to set up bank or investment accounts or enter into any transactions of tax-reporting consequence (such as a sale or purchase), the estate must have its own EIN. Court documents frequently request the EIN, as well. You will use this number for any bank accounts you open for the estate's use of the estate — at minimum, a checking account — and for filing any estate-tax returns.

Apply for an EIN as soon as the court makes your appointment as personal representative official. You can get an EIN by contacting the IRS at 1-800-829-4933, or online at **www.irs.gov/businesses**. You cannot use the deceased person's identification number for the estate, even if he or she had a business EIN.

Closing the loop on tax obligations is part of your fiduciary responsibility. Failure to file a tax return can result in penalties, which deplete the estate's assets. You may be able to avoid penalties by showing you filed late because of a circumstance the IRS accepts as "reasonable." Delegating the task to an attorney, accountant, or other professional is not a reasonable cause for late filing, according to the IRS, although the professional may be liable for malpractice. Ultimately, you are responsible for ensuring that all tax requirements are satisfied.

Frequently Asked Questions on Estate Taxes from the IRS

The following questions and answers on gift taxes are from the IRS. You can find more information by visiting **www.irs.gov/businesses/small/article/0,,id=164871,00.html.**

When can I expect the Estate Tax Closing Letter?

There can be some variation, but for returns that are accepted as filed and contain no other errors or special circumstances, you should expect to wait about four to six months after the return is filed to receive your closing letter. Returns that are selected for examination or reviewed for statistical purposes will take longer.

What is included in the estate?

The gross estate of the decedent consists of an accounting of everything you own or have certain interests in at the date of death. The fair market value of these items is used, not necessarily what you paid for them or what their values were when you acquired them. The total of all of these items is your "gross estate." The includible property may consist of cash and securities, real estate, insurance, trusts, annuities, business interests, and other assets. Keep in mind that the gross estate will likely include non-probate as well as probate property.

I own a 1/2 interest in a farm (or building, or business) with my brother (sister, friend, other). What is included?

Depending on how your 1/2 interest is held and treated under state law, and how it was acquired, you would probably only include 1/2 of its value in your gross estate. However, many other factors influence this answer, so you would need to visit with a tax or legal professional to make that determination.

What is excluded from the estate?

Generally, the gross estate does not include property owned solely by the decedent's spouse or other individuals. Lifetime gifts that are complete (no powers or other control over the gifts are retained) are not included in the gross estate (but, taxable gifts are used in the computation of the estate tax). Life estates given to the decedent by others in which the decedent has no further control or power at the date of death are not included.

What deductions are available to reduce the estate tax?

1. Marital deduction: One of the primary deductions for married decedents is the marital deduction. All property that is included in the gross estate and passes to the surviving spouse is eligible for the marital deduction. The property must pass "outright." In some cases, certain life estates also qualify for the marital deduction.

2. Charitable deduction: If the decedent leaves property to a qualifying charity, it is deductible from the gross estate.

3. Mortgages and debt.

4. Administration expenses of the estate.

5. Losses during estate administration.

What other information do I need to include with the return?

Among other items listed:

1. Copies of the death certificate.

2. Copies of the decedent's will and/or relevant trusts.

3. Copies of appraisals.

4. Copies of relevant documents regarding litigation involving the estate.

5. Documentation of any unusual items shown on the return (partially included assets, losses, near date-of-death transfers, others).

What is "fair market value?"

Fair market value is defined as "the price at which the property would change hands between a willing buyer and a willing seller, neither being under any compulsion to buy or to sell, and both having reasonable knowledge of relevant facts. The fair market value of a particular item of property includible in the decedent's gross estate is not to be determined by a forced sale price. Nor is the fair market value of an item of property to be determined by the sale price of the item in a market other than that in which such item is most commonly sold to the public, taking into account the location of the item wherever appropriate." Regulation §20.2031-1.

What about the value of my family business/farm?

Generally, the fair market value of such interests owned by the decedent are includible in the gross estate at the date of death. However, for certain farms or businesses operated as a family farm or business, reductions to these amounts may be available.

In the case of a qualifying Family Farm, IRC §2032A allows a reduction from value of up to $820,000.

If the decedent owned an interest in a qualifying family-owned business, a deduction from the gross estate in the amount of up to $1,100,000 may be available under IRC §2057.

What if I do not have everything ready for filing by the due date?

The estate's representative may request an extension of time to file for up to six months from the due date of the return. However, the correct amount of tax is still due by the due date, and interest is accrued on any amounts still owed by the due date that are not paid at that time.

Who should I hire to represent me and prepare and file the return?

The Internal Revenue Service cannot make recommendations about specific individuals, but here are some factors to consider:

1. How complex is the estate? By the time most estates reach $1,000,000, there is usually some complexity involved.

2. How large is the estate?

3. In what condition are the decedent's records?

4. How many beneficiaries are there, and are they cooperative?

5. Do I need an attorney, CPA, Enrolled Agent (EA), or other professional(s)?

With these questions in mind, it is a good idea to discuss the matter with several attorneys and CPAs or EAs. Ask about how much experience they have had and ask for referrals. This process should be similar to locating a good physician. Locate other individuals that have had similar experiences and ask for recommendations. Finally, after the individual(s) are employed and begin to work on estate matters, make sure the lines of communication remain open so that there are no surprises during administration or if the estate tax return is examined.

Finally, most estates engage the services of both attorneys and CPAs or EAs. The attorney usually handles probate matters and reviews the impact of documents on the estate tax return. The CPA or EA often handles the actual return preparation and some representation of the estate in matters with the IRS. However, some attorneys handle all of the work. CPAs and EAs may also handle most of the work, but cannot take care of probate matters and other situations where a law license is required. In addition, other professionals (such as appraisers, surveyors, financial advisors, and others) may need to be engaged during this time.

Do I have to talk to the IRS during an examination?

You do not have to be present during an examination unless an IRS representative needs to ask specific questions. Although you may represent yourself during an examination, most executors prefer that professional(s) they have employed handle this phase of administration. They may delegate authority for this by signing a designation on the Form 706 itself, or executing Form 2848 "Power of Attorney."

What if I disagree with the examination proposals?

You have many rights and avenues of appeal if you disagree with any proposals made by the IRS.

What happens if I sell property that I have inherited?

The sale of such property is usually considered the sale of a capital asset and may be subject to capital gains (or loss) treatment. However, IRC §1014 provides that the basis of property acquired from a decedent is its fair market value at the date of death, so there is usually little or no gain to account for if the sale occurs soon after the date of death. (Remember, the rules are different for determining the basis of property received as a lifetime gift.)

Request for Discharge from Personal Liability

Once you determine, file, and pay (if due) any taxes for the estate, you can make a written request for discharge from personal liability for these taxes. Clearly state that your request is for discharge from personal liability under section 6905 of the Internal Revenue Code and that you are appointed, qualified, or acting within the United States.

If additional taxes are due, the IRS will notify you of the remaining amount within nine months after receiving the request. Upon paying this amount, you will not be held personally liable for any future deficiencies. If the IRS does not notify you, you will be discharged from personal liability at the end of the nine-month period.

Insolvent Estate

Even if an estate is unable to pay all the deceased person's debts, you must still pay certain debts first. The deceased person's federal income-tax liabilities at the time of death and the estate's income-tax liability are debts that are due to the IRS. If you are the personal representative for an insolvent estate, you are responsible for any tax liability of the deceased person or of the estate if you knew about those obligations, or did not take adequate steps to find out whether such obligations existed before you distributed the estate's assets and were discharged from your duties.

The extent of your responsibility is the amount of payments you made to other people before you paid the debts due to the United States, except when the other debts have priority. The income-tax debts do not need to be formally evaluated for you to be liable if you knew about or should have known of their existence.

CASE STUDY: TAXES AND
GIFTS: THE MYSTERIES

David J. Bernstein, Attorney at Law
33111 Seneca Drive
Solon, Ohio 44139
(440) 349-4889
Web site: www.estatefacts.com

The tax laws are not designed to protect your estate. Instead, they are designed to take away from your estate as much as possible in order to raise revenue for the federal and state governments. The estate laws of each state do provide some protection to you, but they are designed to put the rights of your creditors first and your beneficiaries last. A competent estate-planning attorney can design your estate plan to minimize taxes and preserve as much of your estate as possible.

As technology has advanced, the process for estate planning has become easier and simpler. Estate planning professionals typically have your estate plan fully in place in just a few days or weeks. The client's time can be minimized to just a few hours.

One of the big mistakes that I see in estate plans is to leave a single dollar to someone to whom you do not want to leave anything. This is not the right way to do this. It may cost thousands of dollars for the administrator to hire an investigator to track down an estranged heir to deliver the single dollar. The best language is to name the person being left out and state that they are intentionally omitted. Stating the reason could lead to a successful challenge if it is not worded properly, so it is better not to state the reason. Disinherited persons may wish to contest not being included, but they must prove that you were incompetent or unaware of your family, environment, or estate, or that there was fraud, mistake, or undue influence at the time you signed the estate plan. Without one or more of these elements, they have no hope of winning.

For gifts, the right choice to go with is dependent on what the client wants to see happen. I tell my clients that they do not know how much money they will need to live on for the rest of their lives. If they start giving it away before they die, it may not be available in a time of need. Gifting is typically only best for the very wealthy who know that their financial needs will be met no matter what happens.

There is plenty of hope if planning takes place before your incapacity. You can hand-pick who will take over, without interference of any outsider. If no plan is in place at the time of your incapacity, you may find yourself at the discretion of the probate court and a court-appointed guardian (who may also be a probate attorney), which could cost your estate tens of thousands of dollars per year.

Estate Income Taxes

Because it is an entity, an estate can generate income that is subject to its own income tax. The IRS even has a form for this — "Income Tax Return of an Estate – Form 1041."

As noted, the estate becomes available upon a person's death and is its own entity with its own EIN. It exists until its assets are fully and completely distributed to heirs and beneficiaries. If income is accrued by the assets during this period, the estate must report it. Not all estates generate income. However, if they do, the tax is figured in the same way as for individuals, with certain differences in figuring deductions and credits.

You must report the estate's income annually on either a calendar- or fiscal-year basis. You will choose the accounting period when filing the estate's first Form 1041. Once you choose the tax year, you cannot change it without IRS approval.

A Form 1041 must be filed for every domestic estate with gross income of $600 or more during a tax year. The personal representative must file a separate form, called a Schedule K-1, for each beneficiary. These forms are to be filed along with Form 1041. The K-1 must include each beneficiary's taxpayer identification number. Failure to do this will result in a $50 penalty for each beneficiary.

Thus, when you take on the duties of personal representative, it is your job to ask each beneficiary for a taxpayer identification number.

You also must provide the beneficiary with the Schedule K-1 by the date the Form 1041 is filed. Failure to do this also can result in a $50 penalty.

If an estate has two or more personal representatives — as is often the case when the property is located in a different state than where the deceased person's home was — each representative must file a separate Form 1041 with the appropriate IRS office for his or her location, assuming the estate has reportable income.

Sources of taxable estate income include:

- Bank account or other investment interest
- Proceeds from sale of property — capital gain

Likewise, offsets to income can include capital losses, expenses, and deductions. Consult with a tax adviser for the estate income-tax return if you are not a tax expert yourself.

Charitable Contributions

One question that sometimes arises is whether the estate qualifies for a deduction for amounts of gross income paid or allocated permanently for charitable organizations. The adjusted gross income limits for individuals do not apply to estates, though. To be deductible by an estate, a charitable contribution must be specifically included in the deceased person's will. In the case that there is no will, or if the will makes no provision for the donation, the IRS does not allow a deduction even though all the beneficiaries may agree to the gift. In other words, charitable deductions do not reduce the taxable size of an estate.

Administration Expenses

You can deduct the expenses of administering an estate either from the gross estate in figuring the federal estate tax or from the estate's gross income, although not for both. Be sure the accountant or tax expert advising you is aware of these expenses.

Depending on the estate's size, other items on the tax checklist can include accrued estate expenses, depreciation and depletion of property values that accrue after the deceased person's death and before final distribution of the estate, capital gains or losses, and other expenses and costs incurred by the estate.

Funeral and Medical Expenses

You cannot take a deduction for funeral and medical or dental expenses on the estate's income tax return. These expenses count against the estate's net value.

Tax Payments

You must pay the estate's income-tax liability in full when you file the return. You may also have to pay estimated tax. Estates must pay estimated tax in the same manner as individuals do if the estate has a tax year ending two or more years after the death date of the deceased person.

You may face a penalty for not paying the correct estimated tax or for not making the payment on time in the adequate amount, even if the tax return indicates an overpayment. This is another risk that underscores the importance of using the advice and services of someone whose business is preparing tax returns. It is a legitimate cost of the estate and is in its best fiduciary interest.

Gift Taxes

The gift tax is a tax on the transfer of property by one individual to another while receiving nothing, or less than full value, in return. The tax applies whether the donor intends the transfer to be a gift or not. To be subject to a gift tax in 2010, the giver must give a gift that exceeds the annual cap of $13,000 per person annually. The gift tax is not imposed on most gifts, and most estates are not subject to the estate tax. Gifts that go to a spouse or to a charity after the deceased person's death are not usually taxed. Gifts that go to someone else are not usually subject to the gift tax unless the value surpasses the annual exclusion for the year.

Even when taxes are applied to gifts and the estate, the unified credit might reduce or eliminate them.

A unified credit applies to the gift tax and the estate tax by subtracting the credit from any gift tax that a person owes. The unified credit used against the gift tax one year reduces the amount of credit that can be used against the gift tax in a later year. By determining which gifts are taxable, the unified credit for the year is figured out against the amount of the gift tax on the total taxable gifts. The credit you can use against the estate tax is reduced by the total amount against your gift tax. The unified credit against taxable gifts will remain $345,800 through 2009. The unified credit against the estate tax was $1,455,800 in 2009.

Transferring any type of property is subject to the gift tax. A person makes a gift by giving property, including money, or using income from a property without intending to get anything in return. You may also be making a gift by selling something at less than half of its value, or by making an interest-free or reduced-interest loan.

Frequently Asked Questions on Gift Taxes from the IRS

The following questions and answers on gift taxes are from the IRS. You can find out more information by visiting **www.irs.gov/businesses/small/ article/0,,id=164872,00.html.**

Who pays the gift tax?

The donor is generally responsible for paying the gift tax. Under special arrangements, the donee may agree to pay the tax instead. Please visit with your tax professional if you are considering this type of arrangement.

What is considered a gift?

Any transfer to an individual, either directly or indirectly, where full consideration (measured in money or money's worth) is not received in return.

What can be excluded from gifts?

The general rule is that any gift is a taxable gift. However, there are many exceptions to this rule. Generally, the following gifts are not taxable gifts:

1. Gifts that are not more than the annual exclusion for the calendar year.

2. Tuition or medical expenses you pay for someone (the educational and medical exclusions).

3. Gifts to your spouse.

4. Gifts to a political organization for its use.

In addition to this, gifts to qualifying charities are deductible from the value of the gift(s) made.

May I deduct gifts on my income tax return?

Making a gift or leaving your estate to your heirs does not ordinarily affect your federal income tax. You cannot deduct the value of gifts you make (other than gifts that are deductible charitable contributions). If you are not sure whether the gift tax or the estate tax applies to your situation, refer to Publication 950, Introduction to Estate and Gift Taxes.

How many annual exclusions are available?

The annual exclusion applies to gifts to each donee. In other words, if you give each of your children $11,000 in 2002 to 2005, $12,000 in 2006 to 2008, and $13,000 on or after January 1, 2009, the annual exclusion applies to each gift.

What if my spouse and I want to give away property that we own together?

You are each entitled to the annual exclusion amount on the gift. Together, you can give $22,000 to each donee (2002 to 2005) or $24,000 (2006 to 2008), $26,000 (effective on or after January 1, 2009).

What other information do I need to include with the return?

Refer to Form 709, 709 Instructions, and Publication 950. Among other items listed:

1. Copies of appraisals.

2. Copies of relevant documents regarding the transfer.

3. Documentation of any unusual items shown on the return (partially gifted assets or other items relevant to the transfer(s)).

What is "fair market value?"

Fair market value is defined as "the price at which the property would change hands between a willing buyer and a willing seller, neither being under any compulsion to buy or to sell and both having reasonable knowledge of relevant facts. The fair market value of a particular item of property includible in the decedent's gross estate is not to be determined by a forced sale price. Nor is the fair market value of an item of property to be determined by the sale price of the item in a market other than that in which such item is most commonly sold to the public, taking into account the location of the item wherever appropriate." Regulation §20.2031-1.

Who should I hire to represent me and prepare and file the return?

The Internal Revenue Service cannot make recommendations about specific individuals, but there are several factors to consider:

1. How complex is the transfer?

2. How large is the transfer?

3. Do I need an attorney, CPA, Enrolled Agent (EA), or other professional(s)?

For most simple, small transfers (less than the annual exclusion amount), you may not need the services of a professional.

However, if the transfer is large or complicated, or both, these actions should be considered; it is a good idea to discuss the matter with several attorneys and CPAs or EAs. Ask about how much experience they have had and ask for referrals. This process should be similar to locating a good physician. Locate other individuals that have had similar experiences and ask for recommendations. Finally, after the individual(s) are employed and begin to work on transfer matters, make sure the lines of communication remain open so that there are no surprises.

Finally, people who make gifts as a part of their overall estate and financial plan often engage the services of both attorneys and CPAs, EAs, and other professionals. The attorney usually handles wills, trusts, and transfer documents that are involved, and reviews the impact of documents on the gift tax return and overall plan. The CPA or EA often handles the actual return preparation and some representation of the donor in matters with the IRS. However, some attorneys handle all of the work. CPAs may also handle most of the work, but cannot take care of wills, trusts, deeds, and other matters where a law license is required. In addition, other professionals (such as appraisers, surveyors, financial advisors, and others) may need to be engaged during this time.

Do I have to talk to the IRS during an examination?

You do not have to be present during an examination unless IRS representatives need to ask specific questions. Although you may represent yourself during an examination, most donors prefer that the professional(s) they have employed handle this phase of the examination. You may delegate authority for this by executing Form 2848 "Power of Attorney."

What if I disagree with the examination proposals?

You have many rights and avenues of appeal if you disagree with any proposals made by the IRS.

What if I sell property that has been given to me?

The general rule is that your basis in the property is the same as the basis of the donor. For example, if you were given stock that the donor had purchased for $10 per share (and that was his/her basis) and you later sold it for $100 per share, you would pay income tax on a gain of $90 per share. (Note: The rules are different for property acquired from an estate.)

Filing Estate and Gift Tax Returns

When to File

Generally, the estate tax return is due nine months after the date of death. A six-month extension is available if requested prior to the due date and the estimated correct amount of tax is paid before the due date.

The gift tax return is due on April 15 of following the year in which the gift is made.

Where to File

Use the below mailing address for all tax forms filed at the Cincinnati Service Center, including Estate and Gift tax returns:

Internal Revenue Service
Cincinnati, OH 45999

To mail FedEx packages, please use the following street address:

Internal Revenue Service
201 W. Rivercenter Blvd.
Covington, KY 41011

Contact Information

For questions about return accounts and extensions only, (no tax law questions) call: (866) 699-4083.

Many general estate and gift tax law questions can still be answered by calling: (800) 829-1040.

Caution: Do not submit tax-related questions below. If you have a tax question, please call our toll-free tax assistance line at 1-800-829-1040 for individual tax questions, or 1-800-829-4933 for business tax questions.

CHAPTER 11

Final Filing Requirements

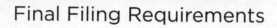

All personal representatives must include the fees from an estate that were paid to them in their own gross income, according to the IRS. Self-employment tax may also apply to such fees if you are a professional personal representative (someone who makes a living representing estates).

For a nonprofessional personal representative, self-employment applies only if the estate's assets include a trade or business, if the personal representative actively takes part in the business, and if the fees are related to the business' undertakings. A nonprofessional personal representative is someone who performs administrative duties only for that particular estate and does not make his or her regular living doing so. This is often a friend or relative of the deceased person.

Information on these issues is available from the IRS in its Publication 559, "Survivors, Executors and Administrators," and Publication 950, "Introduction to Estate and Gift Taxes."

Final Return for Deceased Person

As noted in Chapter 10, the personal representative (possibly in conjunction with a surviving spouse) must file the deceased person's final income-tax return for the year of death, as well as any returns not filed for earlier years. If a person dies after the close of the tax year, but before he or she could file a tax return for that year, you will need to file both that return and an additional "final" return for the deceased person, if IRS rules require it. A deceased person's gross income, age, and filing status (married or single) determine if a return must be filed or not.

You do not need to file a death certificate with the return, but you will need to include your letter of authority from the court. For more information, see the income-tax return instructions or IRS Publication 501, "Exemptions, Standard Deduction, and Filing Information."

Refund

Even if IRS criteria indicate that you are not required to file a return for the deceased person, you should still do it to obtain a refund if tax was withheld from wages, salaries, pensions, or annuities, or if estimated tax was paid. Also, the deceased person may be eligible for other credits resulting in refunds.

If you are a surviving spouse and you receive a tax-refund check in both your deceased spouse's and your name, the check can be reissued in just your name. Simply return the check that has both names along with a completed IRS Form 1310 — Statement of Person Claiming Refund Due a Deceased Taxpayer — to your local IRS office or the service center where you mailed your return. Expect a new check in the mail issued in your name.

Nonresident alien

If the deceased person was a nonresident alien who would have had to file Form 1040-NR, U.S. Nonresident Alien Income Tax Return, you must file that form for the final tax year of the deceased person. Look at the instructions for Form 1040-NR which lay out the filing requirements, due date, and where to file.

Joint return

The surviving spouse and the personal representative usually can file a joint return for the deceased person and spouse. If a personal representative has not been selected before the due date for filing the final joint return for the year of death, then the surviving spouse can file the joint return alone. This is also applicable to the tax return for the preceding year if the deceased person died after the close of the tax year, but before filing the return for that same year.

You cannot file a final joint return for the deceased person if the surviving spouse remarried before the end of the same year in which the deceased person died. In this instance, the filing status of the deceased person would be "married filing a separate return." You can find more information about tax benefits related to a surviving spouse in IRS Publication 559, "Survivors, Executors and Administrators."

Under the cash method

When accounting for income in filing the deceased person's final return, follow his or her prior practice (assuming it was done appropriately). If the deceased person used the cash method to account for income, only include in the final return those items that were actually or constructively (deemed) received before death.

Accrual method

Income is reported as it is earned under the accrual method of accounting. If the deceased person used an accrual method, you will include in the final tax return only the income items normally accumulated before death.

Partnership income

A partner's death closes the partnership's tax year for that one partner only. It does not close the partnership's tax year for the surviving partners. Technically, when a member of a partnership dies, the remaining entity becomes a new partnership.

You must figure the deceased person's distributive share of partnership items as if the partnership's tax year ended on the date of death. To avoid an interim closing of the partnership books, the partners can prorate the amounts the deceased partner would have included for the entire partnership tax year, which would estimate the deceased person's distributive share.

On the deceased person's final return, include the distributive share of partnership items for these periods: the tax year for the partnership that ended within or with the deceased person's final tax year, which is the year ending on the date of death; and the period, if any, from the end of the partnership's tax year to the date of death.

S Corporation income

If the deceased person was a shareholder in an S Corporation, include his or her share of the S Corporation's income, losses, credits, and deductions for the following periods on the final return: the corporation's tax year that ended within or with the deceased person's final tax year, which is the year that ends on the date of death; and the period, if any, from the end of the tax year of the corporation to the death date.

Self-employment income

Depending on the deceased person's accounting method, include actually or constructively acquired or received self-employment income. For self-employment tax purposes only, income will include the deceased person's distributive share of a partnership's loss or income through the end of the month in which he or she died. For this purpose, the partnership's loss or income is considered to be earned ratably over the partnership's tax year.

Community income

If the deceased person lived in a community-property state and had been married, half of the expenses paid and half of the income received during the tax year by either the deceased person or spouse may be considered the expenses and income of the other. You can find more information about this in IRS Publication 555, "Community Property."

Interest and dividend income (Forms 1099)

You will include dividends earned before death on the deceased person's final tax return. These are reported on Forms 1099. If the forms do not correctly reflect the recipient or amounts, you can request corrected Forms 1099.

For example, a Form 1099-INT reporting interest payable to the deceased person may include income that should be reported on the deceased person's final income-tax return. The form may also contain income that the estate or another recipient should report, either as income earned after death or as income in respect of the deceased person. For income earned after death, ask the payer for a Form 1099-INT that properly identifies the recipient by name and identification number, with the correct amount included. If that is not possible, you will have to determine how to allocate the amount.

Other Tax Information

You must be aware of and account for other potential tax information. You may need to do some financial detective work to make sure you have collected everything. This can include health accounts, savings accounts, rent payments, and incidental sources of income.

Additional concerns include accelerated death benefits, medical expenses, exemptions, deductions, losses, extension times, distributions to beneficiaries, education accounts, and retirement accounts.

Talk to a tax adviser to find out how these items affect the tax picture for the deceased person's return and the estate's return.

Extension of time to file

You can request an automatic six-month extension for filing the estate tax return, but keep in mind that this extension does not extend the due date of any taxes owed. You will have to make an estimated payment of what the estate owes. Again, be aware that estate tax laws may be changing. Consult with an expert on these matters.

CHAPTER 12

The Trust Instrument

When first reviewing the trust document, the trustee must understand his or her rights and responsibilities in administering the trust. The agreement should explain in detail the power of the grantor (also called a creator, trustor, or settler), the rights of the beneficiaries and powers of the trustee, assets transferred to and held by the trust, distribution provisions, special provisions, and how and when the trust is to be terminated.

Review the Trust Document

Even before accepting the role of trustee, you should be aware of what is expected of this position. Ask the grantor for a detailed look at the trust document before making a decision and signing it. This is also a good time to make suggestions about the trustee's responsibilities and compensation.

Problems may arise when a grantor does not want to share private issues with a trustee until certain services are actually needed.

Privacy is likely be an important matter to most grantors when it comes to the trust estate and its functions. You should at least ask for general information in such cases so you can provide for a better administration of the estate. If the grantor is reluctant to share details before you commit to the trust, a confidentiality agreement may make him or her more comfortable with the proceedings and will provide you with the information you need to assess whether to take on the role of trustee.

Certain details, such as tax advantages and legal matters, are not as much of a concern to the trustee as the grantor's intentions through the trust instrument. You need to clear up any possible misunderstandings or lack of clarity in the wording as far as managing the estate. If the grantor is unable to address your concerns, you should have a joint meeting with the grantor and his or her lawyer to make sure there is no confusion involving legal matters.

The grantor or an authorized attorney-in-fact should sign the trust agreement. It should be dated, witnessed, and notarized in accordance with state law.

Most trusts are similar in the way they are formatted. The detailed instructions of each trust instrument, however, vary because of the different intentions of each grantor. Understanding the trust document, whether you are a grantor, beneficiary, or trustee, makes it much easier when beginning the administration of the trust.

Many trust instruments begin with a few paragraphs of introduction. This part reveals the grantor establishing the trust, identifies the trustee, and describes the grantor's intent for the trust. An attorney preparing the trust document usually signs it at the top so it can be officially recorded. The trust's tax identification number is also included on the first page. The IRS provides the number when the grantor completes Form SS-4 (Application for Employer Identification Number) and sends it to an IRS office for assignment. The name of the trust is generally identified as the grantor's last name, making it easier for banks, accountants, attorneys, and other professionals to handle matters relating to the trust. A name that describes the trust's function also makes it easier for family members and professionals to work with the trust, especially if a grantor has several trusts.

The date of the trust is very important to include in the first paragraph of the agreement. Assets cannot be transferred to the trust prior to that date, the trust cannot conduct business prior to the date, and tax results often depend on the date the trust officially begins.

When the grantor wants to make gifts to a trust prior to the end of the year, the trust must be established before then. Set up the trust far enough in advance of the end of the year so bank accounts can be opened and initial deposits can be made. If a trust date is too close to the end of the year, it is possible that deadlines will not be met when transferring funds to the trust before year's end. A trust should not list a date after the date of a grantor's will when pour-over provisions are included in a revocable living trust. Pour-over assets included in a will transfer assets to the trust, and the trust document contains details of how the trustee will distribute the assets.

The grantor is the person setting up and endowing the trust. For most trusts, the grantor should not serve as trustee or successor trustee. This is for tax purposes so that the trust's assets are not included in the grantor's estate. In certain irrevocable trusts, such as trusts for insurance or children, the grantor also should not be a beneficiary of the trust.

The grantor's powers are usually very restrictive. In many irrevocable trusts, the grantor may be able to replace a trustee with another trustee. In many revocable trusts, the grantor retains sufficient powers over the trust and property transferred to it. It all depends on the trust's objectives and goals. For an asset protection trust, the grantor may have limited powers to protect assets from creditors. In a revocable living trust, the grantor will want control over the trust and will want to include assets in the estate for beneficial tax purposes.

Transfer of Assets

The transfer of assets to the trust is an essential part of the trust agreement. These are assets that you, as trustee, will hold. The process may require deeds to transfer real estate, sales, tangible property, or various accounts. The grantor should be careful in making decisions about transfers, especially when income, gift- and estate-tax issues, asset protection, and other matters are concerned. The grantor must also carefully consider whether to allow other people (named in the agreement) to contribute to the trust. The grantor should make these instructions clear to you so you can reject assets that may have negative tax or legal consequences.

Selecting the transfer of assets to an estate is obviously important to the grantor, who needs to make these decisions with care. It is an essential part of your duties as trustee to examine these instructions thoroughly when reading the trust document. Not all trusts have assets funded to them. Unfunded trusts are set up to be funded at a later date with assets from the estate. In funded trusts, assets are usually transferred immediately or in the near future. Assets should be listed in the trust document or attached to it as property of the trust. Some assets must be formally transferred to the trust. For example, real estate transfers would need a new deed completed to name the trust as owner.

The trustee should sign partnership agreements and attach them to the document. In these cases, the agreement also needs to name the trust as the owner. Assets transferred to the trust may include tangible or intangible real or personal property. This would include real estate, bank accounts, stocks, securities, partnerships or limited liability company interests, furniture, art, jewelry, and other personal property.

All trusts include the names of people who will benefit from the trust during its term. Identifying the beneficiaries may be very simple. It also can get complex when mentioning primary and succeeding beneficiaries. This setup may occur when the grantor wants assets to be transferred to another beneficiary if one beneficiary dies. The trust agreement may include certain rights and demands by beneficiaries. It also may name groups of beneficiaries, instructing the trustee how and when to distribute income and assets.

The agreement's provisions include the powers, rights, and administrative obligations of the trustee or trustees. Sometimes, the grantor selects a trust protector. The protector is often considered to be an intermediary between the beneficiaries and the trustee. When necessary, a trust protector may act when he or she believes a new trustee should be chosen or thinks there should be a change in location for the trust. The trust protector may even have a limited power to add or change the beneficiaries of the trust. Beneficiaries also are often given the power to change trustees.

As a trustee, you will need a broad range of powers to operate the trust effectively in accordance with the grantor's instructions. You have the power to allocate income and assets to the beneficiaries. Sometimes, you also have the power to withhold distribution of income, especially if the beneficiary is a child or is disabled.

Certain trust documents may be very complex with multiple beneficiaries who have different interests. You may have to use income and principal for the benefit of the grantor's incapacitated spouse, and at the same time provide income instructions for the surviving spouse. You may face decisions about the spouse's health and well-being, while also being concerned about a child's educational needs. These decisions will affect your distribution of assets. The availability of income will play a key role in these choices.

When reviewing the trust document, you should ask the grantor to make clear what wishes and needs are appropriate to provide for if the instructions do not completely spell it out. An attorney for the grantor can also help define the instructions to be certain you make the correct decisions for the trust when the time comes.

Everyone involved should ask the grantor what preferences and details should receive priority. Language in the trust document should be comprehensible so you, as trustee, can handle the estate and assets with better authority. You should be certain that everyone involved understands all definitions of words in the instructions.

State laws include definitions that the trust document does not have to repeat, but many attorneys include the provisions anyway to avoid consulting state authorities. This, of course, changes if the trust moves to another state.

Income-tax planning is often an important part of any trust on both the state and federal levels. Sometimes it can include complicated instructions involving the various deductions and credits allowed to a grantor, depending on the situation. Whether or not the trustee is a tax expert, the grantor should define in the written instructions all terms related to tax considerations.

The trust document will not deal with everyone who has an interest in estate assets. The document may include instructions for an accountant or financial adviser about certain investments or business interests. It may also make references to certain assets that are to go to certain beneficiaries. Often, following the distribution of specified assets, the trust may stipulate that the remaining assets of the estate go to a particular person or persons.

Dispositive provisions, or provisions concerned with the trust's purpose, often identify the beneficiaries who are to receive benefits currently or at some future date. These provisions should instruct you, as trustee, on whether the beneficiaries have absolute rights to benefits, or whether you can make payments at your discretion.

The trust document sometimes does not identify beneficiaries by name, but instead refers to them as "children" or "grandchildren." Talk with an attorney about what these definitions may mean and the legal issues that might affect beneficiaries in the future.

Distributions are made to beneficiaries based on the terms described in the written instructions. As trustee, you may make regular income payments; use principal to make payments when you deem it appropriate; or make payments during certain events, such as a beneficiary reaching adulthood. You should properly identify the beneficiaries and comply with tax-reporting requirements when making required distributions. For example, if you need to distribute income when a beneficiary reaches a certain age, you should verify age by having the beneficiary furnish a birth certificate or other proof.

The trust may instruct you to make distributions at your own discretion. This is when your best judgment will come into play. In such cases, you will have to make your own decisions about a certain beneficiary's needs or support. Sometimes, you may need to weigh the request for income from one beneficiary against the needs of an incapacitated beneficiary or the maintenance of the estate.

Administrative provisions define what you can do with the estate's property and assets, what actions you must perform, and what you cannot do. Grantors may feel strongly about where you should or should not make certain investments. Specific instructions may outline when or where you should make transactions. For example, you may have to compromise claims made against the trust. You should settle such claims as soon as possible with the full benefit of the beneficiaries in mind. You have a duty to make the trust property produce income. You can sell property or assets for cash or credit unless the terms of the trust prohibit it. The trust may have a provision that calls for the retention of property. Whatever the case, if you are considering a sale of real property, the trust document should point out that a sale is permitted.

You will incur expenses when carrying out the trust's instructions. The trust usually includes an expense-allocation provision to provide flexibility when paying out income or principal.

Sometimes, state law limits the way you can distribute certain property from the trust. The instructions may include provisions that direct you to distribute in cash or in kind. For example, you may be able to distribute property to beneficiaries from the property itself or in cash proceeds from the sale of it, whichever the beneficiary prefers, as long as it is under the terms of the trust. You also may be instructed to pay bills on a regular basis for a beneficiary who is mentally or physically disabled. A continuance of status for beneficiaries clause will relieve you of liability if the trust instructions include it. You may not borrow money or mortgage or pledge property to obtain a loan unless the trust specifically mentions it. If you must be involved in companies, the trust might include a provision for dealing with foreclosures, mergers, and reorganizations. This will allow you to carry out certain duties, such as voting as a board member, to make decisions on behalf of a company owned through the trust.

You may be investing assets according to the instructions for the trust. Beneficiaries may want a certain business retained if it keeps them employed. Therefore, the trust may give you the power to retain such property. Instructions may also include provisions that allow you to use your own discretion in disposing of property when it is desirable for the beneficiaries.

Certain state laws may limit your ability to invest in any asset, unless the terms of the trust explain it. The grantor may include a provision for the power to buy and sell at a premium or discount when it comes to investment transactions. This avoids questions as to whether you underpaid or overpaid fees for investments.

The trust also may have a provision for you to employ and retain agents to perform various duties during operation of the trust. The instructions should specifically name the types of agents authorized and address any concerns that state law may restrict in your power to delegate responsibility.

Compensation

Written instructions in the trust document or a separate agreement, as well as state law or a court determination, may set your compensation for serving as trustee. Like the personal representative of an estate, you are entitled to reasonable compensation for your work. Factors included in these fees may include the size of the trust and the income it generates, the extent of your responsibilities, the quality of your work, any problems or difficulties you encounter as trustee, your knowledge and skill as an estate manager, the manner of the estate settlement, and the results. If you are accused of overcharging your fees, use the following factors to defend the costs.

These responsibilities can earn you reasonable compensation:

- Reviewing and adhering to the trust document
- Verifying all of the estate assets and having them transferred into the trust
- Analyzing the assets
- Communicating and discussing matters with beneficiaries
- Determining the needs and benefits of the beneficiaries
- Analyzing and preparing investments
- Planning tax strategies and filing tax returns
- Keeping records and providing beneficiaries with updates
- Preparing and filing accounts
- Dealing with potential liabilities during your term

Discuss compensation with the grantor and agree on fees whenever possible. State laws also set guidelines and regulations for trustee fees. Compensation should be sufficient to provide a fair payment for services and cover any costs not reimbursed by the trust. When determining fees for your work, consider investment management, tax compliances, accounting, and other services. It is possible that you would deserve higher fees than a corporate trustee for a bank or trust company. Personal trustees can farm out services to various professionals that a corporate trustee, who must stay within the framework of the company, cannot. Trustees handling one client also have the advantage of working closely with that client, unlike banks or trust companies that have standardized customer service.

You should charge additional fees for extraordinary services, such as handling the sale of a business or real estate interest, locating missing beneficiaries, or other demanding or time-consuming tasks.

CHAPTER 13

Administering Trusts

A person who is asked to be a trustee has a right to decline the offer. Once you agree to take on the duties of a trustee, you must abide by that agreement. No matter how experienced or inexperienced you are in such a position, you will be held to high standards. You are in a fiduciary relationship with the beneficiaries. Although you can resign from the position if you decide the job is too burdensome, it is better to be absolutely sure you can perform a trustee's required duties before you take on the role. Resignation requires more forms and only takes up more time and effort.

What to Do First

After accepting the appointment, take some basic initial steps as soon as possible. One of these is considering purchasing a bond or insurance policy for your performance as a trustee. This will protect you from losses due to negligence or illegal acts. Some trust agreements may relieve you from being bonded, depending on the circumstances. However, it is always a good idea to be on the safe side. Find an agency that provides fiduciary bonds. The purchase would be an expense of the trust; however, you may have to provide the initial fees if the trust does not have funds available immediately. You can be reimbursed later.

Obtain important documents and hold them securely in a special file. The most important is the trust document or a copy of it, a copy of the grantor's will, or a copy of the court decree ordering the trust. You should also include the original copy of your acceptance of the role of trustee and the original copy of the resignation of the previous trustee, if there was one. Other documents include death certificates, deeds to real property, copies of the federal estate-tax return, copies of receipts for assets received, and a federal employee identification number (EIN) because your role as trustee is now a business. Place personal-loan notes, mortgage notes, accounts receivable papers, documents for patents, and similar documents in a safe-deposit box under the name of the trust.

You should begin gathering assets at the first possible opportunity. Identify all assets belonging to the trust. The difficulty of this task depends on the type of trust or the grantor. If the grantor were alive and competent, it would be easy for you to identify the assets and transfer them to the trust. Some grantors may set up a trust because they are not capable of properly handling assets due to physical or mental ailments. This can make it more difficult for you to gather assets. If you are handling a trust created under a will, you may have to do a lot of homework in determining if all the assets are being received for the trust. You will also have to seek out tax and accounting information to make sure taxes on the assets have been paid, or that the accounting has been done properly.

Checking the tax information and accounting is also a necessity for a successor trustee. Such trustees will often need proof of their authority in dealing with institutions, businesses, and individuals while collecting assets.

In setting up management of the trust, you need a checking account in the trust's name to collect cash balances from other sources, deposit trust income, and pay expenses for the trust. It does not have to be an interest-bearing account because it will be for initial financial transactions and will need only a minimum balance to avoid extra bank charges. You can open a separate interest-bearing account for additional cash. The initial checking account will help you keep records of all deposits and payments, and you can use it as a way to funnel additional monies into interest-bearing accounts or money-market funds.

Keep art, jewelry, stamps, and other collectibles in a safe-deposit vault unless the trust agreement stipulates other arrangements. Be sure to itemize and insure all tangible property. If you need to keep any items in a large facility, such as antique furniture or vehicles, do it in a way that ensures the assets will be safe and insured. When in charge of real estate, you should thoroughly inspect each property and/or arrange for necessary professional inspections. You should immediately identify all repairs and maintenance needed and arrange for the transfer of title. Bills for utility or other property services should be sent to you. If the estate involves business interests, you need to know your responsibilities, most often explained in the trust agreement, and immediately determine your powers in the business, whether acting as owner or being placed on a corporate board.

Check on social security benefits, pension benefits, annuities, or other payments — if the trust includes them — and have them directed to your attention. You will need to maintain a detailed inventory of all trust assets. It should include such information as the date the property was received, as well as its cost or market value on the date it was turned over to the trust.

Your job as a trustee is to manage and dispose of trust assets for the benefit of the grantor. If required by the trust, you also will pay the grantor the net income of the trust and some or all of the principal. If the grantor becomes incapacitated, you must use the income and principal for maintenance of the estate and support of the grantor's health and welfare. When the grantor dies, you must pay remaining trust assets to the estate or to the beneficiaries, according to the trust's instructions.

Communicating

The way you communicate with the grantor and the beneficiaries may very well determine how the administration of the estate works out in the end. When you communicate effectively, you can avoid any damages or claims and even settle issues among beneficiaries. Discuss with the grantor the reasons why he or she arranged for certain provisions to be made for particular beneficiaries, or why money was sent into a trust instead of given directly to the beneficiaries. When you learn more about why and how the trust was created, you can better deal with the beneficiaries when they ask questions or feel dissatisfied with the trust arrangements.

Communicating effectively with the grantor will also help you when it comes to arranging provisions that benefit you in terms of fees or decision-making. In turn, you should explain your intentions of managing the estate so as to avoid a disagreement or friction.

CASE STUDY: POWER OF ATTORNEY

Law Offices of James N. Reyer, P.A.
5301 North Federal Highway, Suite 130
Boca Raton, FL 33487
(561) 241-9003 - voice
(561) 988-9892 -- fax

A power of attorney must be drawn up during the lifetime of the person who wishes to grant this power to another person. The person granting the power must be legally competent when doing so. Once a person becomes incapacitated, it is too late. Hire someone well-versed in legal vocabulary and law to draft the document and ensure that it complies fully with state statutes. For example, many states recognize the concept of the "durable" power of attorney, which remains in full force and effect even after the person granting the power becomes legally incompetent.

Distributing Assets

Trust beneficiaries usually receive regularly scheduled income, discretionary distributions for particular needs, and mandatory distributions that include income when a beneficiary reaches a certain age or at the termination of the trust. Instructions for making distributions should be in the trust document. These decisions should not be left to your judgment unless you have discussed such matters with the grantor, who then writes out the instructions. When making distributions, make sure you are paying the correct beneficiaries, distributing income at the right time, or making payments during a certain event specified in the instructions. Sometimes you may have to use your own judgment for situations the trust did not anticipate, especially if you notice that a beneficiary has been using payments inappropriately. For example, a beneficiary may be squandering money on a foolish venture or spending it unwisely. In such cases, you should consult with an attorney before taking discretionary action.

Discretionary distributions require knowledge and skill when making payments to beneficiaries. The trust includes these distributions because the grantor may feel the beneficiary needs advice from a person with financial expertise. The beneficiary may be incapacitated, a minor, or a spendthrift. Alternatively, the beneficiary may just be someone who does not know how to handle money properly and needs to be protected. The grantor may give you absolute power in handling discretionary distributions, allowing you to determine the amount, timing, and frequency of payments. Alternatively, the trust may place restrictions on you. In either case, you must remain fair and objective when dealing with all beneficiaries. Being loyal to the estate and beneficiaries is important, but so is preserving the trust property.

You often will have to perform a balancing act to keep all beneficiaries satisfied, while understanding the necessity for proper distributions. Unfortunately, a beneficiary may not like the way he or she is treated and may take you to court, regardless of whether or not you have taken reasonable actions. Keep all the written information from trust instructions and communications with the grantor and any attorney. You may have to present this evidence in court. If you are not keeping proper records and accounts, it can result in a financial loss if the court decides you are in error.

You should make discretionary distributions carefully, keeping track of all your decisions and why you made them.

When a beneficiary asks you for a distribution from a beneficiary, it is up to you to understand how much money is needed for the particular activity or service, what it will be specifically used for, when it is to be spent, and how it will be accounted. For example, say a beneficiary asks you for tuition money. You should detail this request in your records. If you decide the request is valid, you should figure out the amount of tuition and related expenses, such as travel. The beneficiary should provide all the information necessary and, in some cases, proof of the transactions. Keep this information in your records. The same holds true for medical services or necessary household goods, repairs, or additions.

Discretionary distributions usually fall into three categories. Full discretion means you could take into account the beneficiary's income or resources, but would not necessarily have to make such a consideration. Discretionary distributions for a specific amount or purpose mean you are prohibited from considering the beneficiary's other sources of income. The trust may have insufficient funds for certain distribution requests. Distributions to supplement support may require you to look into outside sources of income for the beneficiary. You would have to consider those income sources if the beneficiary requests funding for medical or educational service. In this case, you may have the difficult task of explaining to the beneficiary that he or she is financially able to handle the situation and that income in the trust can be better used elsewhere.

Trustee as a Business

Trustees are self-employed individuals in a separate business activity from any other occupation they may be involved in. You cannot share your job as trustee with another company or entity, regardless of any contract, unless you are sharing the administrative position with an appointed co-trustee. It is possible in some cases that you will be in a business that requires a license. A trustee who handles the estate of one person is most likely not in a business. A trustee who is handling a number of unrelated estates is involved in a profession and a business. In that case, you might have to obtain permits for zoning. You also may have to arrange for licenses and inspections, depending on the location. Local governments most likely would handle these requirements, and fees are nominal. If you have any questions, check with local offices that handle businesses.

For business and/or taxing purposes, it might be wise for you to open a separate bank account to handle all fees related to your duties as a personal representative of an estate. Although it is not required legally or otherwise, a separate account keeps all your activities as a trustee in one place away from your personal or other business activities. Whether or not you open a separate account, do not commingle the trust's financial activity with your own money. Opening a separate account with a bank other than your personal bank also prevents the possibility of a single bank confusing the accounts. Have checks returned either by mail or through computer imaging, rather than putting them in a check-safekeeping-type of account where the checks are simply recorded at the bank. Keep up-to-date with all transactions being made through the trust. Keep checkbook records or stubs and statements showing the check numbers and payees.

You should charge appropriate expenses for the trust's administration, unless the grantor's instructions explain it differently. Costs to you as trustee may include court proceedings; hiring professionals needed for estate services; and management, maintenance, and repairs needed for property. Use your best judgment in improving the estate to increase its value when you are considering a sale. Carefully consider any purchases that others might see as questionable to avoid any unnecessary court proceedings. For example, transportation fees may be necessary in cases where you need to travel for the estate's business dealings or communication with beneficiaries. Be certain that these kinds of expenses are strictly used for the benefit and welfare of the estate and nothing else.

Licensing fees and taxes are part of the trustee's cost in his profession. Legal fees for the trust are usually part of the trustee's costs unless accounted for by the trust document or covered by law, but costs to the trustee's business would include seeking an attorney's advice on deciding whether to accept the position as trustee or defending against claims filed by beneficiaries. Office and work supplies, postage, instructive material, computer software, and expenses paid to employees would also be part of the business if you use them for the purposes of managing the estate.

Many states require trustees to be bonded to protect them against personal loss through negligence or something not performed that hurts the estate and the beneficiaries. To protect yourself, you can obtain insurance policies that would cover errors or omissions that affect the estate and can cause financial hazards for you. These policies are similar to property loss or injury insurance, but focus on protecting you, the policyholder, from claims filed against you in court. Attorneys acting as trustees often have some type of insurance to protect them against claims. A co-trustee may also have an insurance policy that protects another trustee handling the estate. This is not always the case, however. Do your homework in this regard and discuss such a policy with an insurance agent.

Unfortunately, if you are the only trustee and are not a professional trustee, you may find obtaining an insurance policy that protects against claims to be expensive and limited in choices for provisions. Trustees for corporations do not usually have this problem because the company can furnish them with the necessary protective measures. The good news is that insurance for quasi-professionals is becoming more acceptable in the insurance field, especially because the number of estate management cases is growing along with the rising number of older people in America. Non-professional trustees argue that they are engaged in a full-time profession that takes a lot of expertise, even if they learn it on the job. Many insurers, however, are concerned about the high risk amateurs present because of the chance they will make mistakes in handling the trust. Until insurance companies begin to change their ways, it may be difficult for you to find the right policy that completely protects you in the administration of the estate. However, you still may be able to get insurance assistance through the grantor. You can request that the grantor make specific provisions within the trust document for the trust to be responsible for premiums on a liability policy.

Another way to deal with expensive insurance is to have other professionals handle many of your trustee duties. Allowing attorneys, financial advisers, tax consultants, and other experts to take care of specific issues involving the estate can not only save you time, but also curtail the possibility of claims. These professionals most likely already have liability policies. Through contracts, you could also require the professionals to have the necessary insurance to protect them from negligence and malpractice. Make certain all professionals you work with are bonded.

Regardless of which route you take, you should always act prudently in handling the estate to avoid any possibility of negligence or claims.

Managing Real Estate and Business

Properties may be kept in trusts if a surviving spouse or children continue to occupy a primary or other residence. The grantor also may have invested in real estate and transferred the property into a revocable living trust. It is usually an easy task for you, as trustee, to look over a residence, but taking care of investment property is most likely a bigger job. Whatever type of property is in the trust, you must manage it to the best of your ability, making sure it has adequate insurance coverage, keeping up with the maintenance and repair, and paying taxes properly.

The trust agreement may or may not include details on how to manage a residence if a family member occupies it. In the case of a surviving spouse, the trust is considered one-half owner of the property. The spouse and the trust would share maintenance fees and other expenses. If the spouse has income from the trust, you could use those funds to pay for expenses. The surviving spouse may be entitled to sell the property, but you also have the responsibility to the other beneficiaries and should make sure it is sold at a fair market value.

Having adequate insurance on the property is extremely important. You should have an insurance policy naming the trust as an additional insured entity. The coverage should be sufficient to protect the property and the trust. Provisions should include replacement of the property at the current market value in the event of a loss. The same as any homeowner, the trust should have liability insurance for protection in case of an unexpected accident on the premises. Think of the trust as if it were a new homeowner — have a complete inspection and appraisal to make sure the insurance coverage is adequate. Depending on the type of property, you should consider including worker's compensation and rent insurance, as well as protection from fire, liability, casualty, natural and civil disturbances, and other unexpected events.

Environmental issues

A major concern when handling real estate is the possibility of having property that is or becomes environmentally contaminated. You can be held responsible for the cleanup under the Comprehensive Environmental Response, Compensation, and Liability Act (CERCLA) of 1980, also known as Superfund. The act gives the federal government the right to clean up contaminated property and recover the costs from potentially responsible persons, which has since come to include individuals and organizations even remotely associated with the property. In 1986, the Superfund Amendments and Reauthorization Act (SARA) went further by including underground storage tanks.

This can be devastating to the trust if an extensive cleanup operation is necessary, and it can be just as distressing to you. A residence may be located on or near a property previously owned by environmentally reckless occupants. That could bring liability to the trust and to you. In the worst-case scenario, it could even wipe out the trust entirely. To make the problem even more severe, it could wreak havoc among the beneficiaries, who become enraged by the loss of their benefits. It might mean that you become solely responsible for the financial damage because of your obligation to take care of the trust. You can become a target for federal action by knowing the trust property was contaminated and doing nothing about it, or even knowing there is a potential liability for environmental cleanup and using trust assets to pay beneficiaries instead of having the grounds inspected and maintained. This is a clear case of better safe than sorry. Consult with specialists who are qualified to examine environmental issues and law.

Not only do federal acts deal with potential liability for trustees, but state laws also hold them accountable for hazardous cleanups. The good news is that some states have enacted laws that can protect you from beneficiaries who resent you spending money on environmental cleanup. These laws authorize you to spend trust money to repair environmental problems. Some laws even protect innocent trustees from personal liability, but this may depend upon the trustee notifying state environmental authorities of a possible hazard. The Asset Conservation Lender Liability and Deposit Insurance Protection Act of 1996 limits the trustee's liability to only the amount of the trust's assets. However, it still holds the trustee liable in cases of avoiding cleanup costs or negligence. To avoid liability, the act essentially states that you should undertake responsive action in respect to CER-CLA, address hazardous conditions legally, monitor and inspect the property, advise all parties in the trust, change the relationship of the trustee to the trust, or resign as the trustee. If you are administering property already contaminated, this also would be taken into consideration.

The laws regarding this issue can get extremely complex. Avoiding the problem would be the best answer and is relatively simple for you, as trustee. If you realize you will hold real estate in the trust, you should require that an environmental risk assessment be made to determine if hazardous conditions exist on the property. If the assessment finds problems, you should require they be taken care of before you accept the position of trustee. If the problems are not resolved, you can refuse to accept the asset in the trust or decline the position of trustee. It would be better for you, the grantor, and all beneficiaries for the trust document to list provisions regarding potential environmental hazards on property. Regardless, you should conduct a thorough evaluation of the property or have an environmental inspection if you suspect any contamination.

Properties that might present potential environmental threats include those on industrial, manufacturing, agricultural, automotive, and other service sites. You may also want to evaluate nearby property if you think hazardous conditions can spread. Businesses that handle hazardous material could cause problems, too. Check on previous owners and find out about their use of the property. If you are handling a property where hazardous chemicals are used, you should check for permits with the Environmental Protection Agency (EPA) and local agencies. You could also obtain an environmental audit, which examines the environmental practices and records of a facility, while making sure the organization adheres to correct environmental policies. When in doubt, check with an environmental specialist or with local and national environmental organizations for advice.

Investment properties

As trustee, you may be called on to supervise investment property. You have a duty to make sure the property remains productive. This may entail making improvements to the property or selling it to invest the proceeds. You also could lease the property or continue operating it as long as it is productive, depending on the instructions in the trust agreement. It is possible a beneficiary would like to use the property and is entitled to income from the trust. This might relieve you of the task of making sure the property keeps earning income. The beneficiary might want to use the land or sell it. How you handle the situation would depend on the trust document and your judgment.

The property could be a residence, small apartment building, condominium complex, or a commercial enterprise. Your decision on what to do with it depends on its condition and the interests of the beneficiaries. If the property promises to be a moneymaking venture for the trust, necessary improvements might be worthwhile. If you cannot make such a decision with certainty, sell the property and use the proceeds for the trust.

Sometimes, you may have to manage property that is out of state. The trust agreement often addresses this situation. If it does not, discuss it with the grantor. A separate trustee could handle the property under the agreement. Managing out-of-state property requires special attention, and you should at least consider hiring a professional manager in the area to supervise the property.

Managing business

You cannot retain a closely held business interest in a trust unless it is specifically authorized under the terms of the trust, under local law, or by court order. Entrepreneurs may see a trust as a way to preserve a business interest with the hope their offspring will continue the enterprise successfully. In most cases, however, ownership of the family business dissipates before the third generation, according to research from the Family Firm Institute.

A business may end up in a trust because the owner is unable to dispose of it before death. A trust can hold a business interest for a family that has the desire to keep it. The business could be the main or only source of income for some family members. As trustee, you will have the task of income production, marketability, valuation, and the daily responsibility of keeping the business in operation, which might be the hardest part. In some cases, the trust is left with a minor interest in the business, and your duties will be passive, such as expressing concerns about business decisions. If the trust has a majority interest, you will be saddled with full involvement with the business. That means overseeing and retaining managers, dealing with the minority interests, or handling the sale of the business, if necessary. You may earn a seat on the board, which could create conflicts between the beneficiaries and other shareholders.

There are reasons for the trust to keep the business. The trust document may specifically state that you should manage the business interest without any liability. The trust may terminate in a short period and the beneficiaries decide to retain interests. The business may also be profitable and easily managed without posing any risks to the trust. Before accepting the job of trustee, you should consider a major evaluation of the business. It should have capable managers, a good return on investment, and the ability to continue with positive future earnings to make it worthwhile for the beneficiaries and remaindermen.

The business interest can be a sole proprietorship, general partnership, limited partnership, C Corporation, S Corporation (named for Subchapter S of the IRS code), or limited liability company (LLC).

Legal Entities 101

Sole proprietorship

Sole proprietorship is the most prevalent type of legal structure adopted by start-up or small businesses, and it is the easiest to put into operation. It is a type of business that is owned and operated by one owner and it is not set up as any kind of corporation. Therefore, you will have absolute control of all operations. Under a sole proprietorship, you own 100 percent of the business, its assets, and its liabilities. Some of the disadvantages are that you are wholly responsible for securing any and all monetary backing, and you are ultimately responsible for any legal actions against your business. However, it has some great advantages, such as being relatively inexpensive to set up, and with the exception of a few extra tax forms, there is no requirement to file complicated tax returns in addition to your own. Also, as a sole proprietor, you can operate under your own name, or you can choose to conduct business under a fictitious name. Most business owners who start small begin their operations as sole proprietors.

General partnership

A partnership is almost as easy to establish as a sole proprietorship, with a few exceptions. In a partnership, all profits and losses are shared among the partners. In a partnership, not all partners necessarily have equal ownership of the business. Normally, the extent of financial contributions toward the business will determine the percentage of each partner's ownership. This percentage relates to sharing the organization's revenues as well as its financial and legal liabilities. One key difference between a partnership and a sole proprietorship is that the business does not cease to exist with the death of a partner. Under such circumstances, the deceased partner's share can either be taken over by a new partner, or the partnership can be reorganized to accommodate the change. In either case, the business is able to continue without much disruption.

Limited liability company

A limited liability company (LLC), often wrongly referred to as limited liability corporation, is not quite a corporation, yet is much more than a partnership. An LLC encompasses features found in the legal structure of corporations and partnerships, which allows the owners — called members in the case of an LLC — to enjoy the same liability protection of a corporation and the record-keeping flexibility of a partnership, like not having to keep meeting minutes or records. In an LLC, the members are not personally liable for the debts incurred for and by the company, and profits can be distributed as deemed appropriate by its members. In addition, all expenses, losses, and profits of the company flow through the business to each member, who would ultimately pay either business taxes or personal taxes — and not both on the same income.

Corporation

Corporations are the most formal type of all the legal business structures discussed so far. A corporation can be established as a public or a private corporation. A public corporation, with which most of us are familiar, is owned by its shareholders (also known as stockholders) and is public because anyone can buy stocks in the company through public stock exchanges. Shareholders are owners of the corporation through the ownership of shares or stocks, which represent a financial interest in the company.

Not all corporations start up as corporations, selling shares in the open market. They may actually start up as individually owned businesses that grow to the point where selling its stocks in the open market is the most financially feasible business move for the organization. However, openly trading your company's shares diminishes your control over it by spreading the decision-making to stockholders or shareholders and a board of directors. Some of the most familiar household names, like the Tupperware Corporation and The Sports Authority, Inc., are public corporations.

S Corporation

An S Corporation is a form of legal structure; under IRS regulations designed for the small businesses — "S Corporation" means small business corporation. Until the inception of the limited liability company form of business structure, forming S Corporations was the only choice available to small business owners, which offered some form of limited liability protection from creditors, yet afforded them with the many benefits that a partnership provides. Operating under S Corporation status results in the company being taxed close to how a partnership or sole proprietor would be taxed, rather than being taxed like a corporation.

Operating under the S Corporation legal structure, the shareholders' taxes are directly impacted by the business's profit or loss. Any profits or losses the company may experience in any one year are passed through to the shareholders who in turn must report them as part of their own income tax returns. According to the IRS, shareholders must pay taxes on the profits the business realized for that year in proportion to the stock they own.

The S Corporation, proprietorship, partnership, and LLC interests have income that is taxed directly to the holder of the interest. The C Corporation pays a tax on earnings as the earnings are paid out to stockholders in dividends. The shareholders again pay income tax on the dividends.

A trustee who becomes owner of a general partnership interest has unlimited liability for the partnership. The general partner has a duty to manage the business in the best interest of the limited partners. You have to manage the partnership in the best interest of the beneficiaries, which could create conflicts of interest. You might consider converting to an LLC or S Corporation.

An S Corporation held in the trust is usually carefully arranged for the estate plans by the grantor. It contains such attributes as unlimited life and limited liability. However, you ensure that this is the case. If the grantor badly planned the arrangement, the intended shareholders may not be eligible, causing problems within and outside the trust. A Qualified Subchapter S Trust (QSST) contains these elements:

- It must be a trust in the United States.
- All income must be distributed.
- There is only one current income beneficiary who must be a U.S. citizen.
- Principal distributions must go to that beneficiary.
- The beneficiary's interest must be for life or the term of the trust.
- The beneficiary must receive all assets in the trust if it ends before he or she dies.

You may have to amend the trust to have the S Corporation status, if you have the authority to do so. If the trust does not allow this provision, you might consider petitioning the court to avoid losing the status.

In an S Corporation, you should determine whether the trust holds a controlling or minority interest. A controlling interest does not necessarily mean owning more than 50 percent of shares in the stock. It could be that the shareholders are the trust's beneficiaries, giving you a stronger holding over the interest. You could serve as officer or director of the company. Naturally, this all depends on the potential liability involved in being a major force in the business. However, maintaining control over the business could be advantageous for beneficiaries.

To avoid any conflicts, you should not accept any fees or compensation from the company for serving as an officer or director. You should receive adequate liability insurance. If you do not want to serve in these positions, you should still attend all shareholder meetings to be informed in case major decisions are necessary. You should monitor all activities in the business and frequently review and evaluate company financial reports, profit and loss statements, spreadsheets, sales reports, and other valuable data. You should visit the business regularly to inspect the operations and keep abreast of conditions.

Selling the business

If proceeds from the business are not an advantage to the trust, and if the trust document and legal order do not make it necessary to retain the business, you should sell it as soon as possible at a fair and reasonable value. It may take a long time to sell a business, and you must keep the business in operation to keep proceeds rolling in during the process. You must preserve the business's value during this time and manage it properly. To avoid any litigation in the meantime, the proper contracts must be agreed upon and signed, maintaining order in the transition.

In some situations, a sale can be easy if the grantor had entered into a buy-sell agreement with a partner or partners. This type of agreement provides for the purchase of the deceased person's interest in the business. It usually establishes the price and allows for value changes as the business grows. As trustee, you must sell the business in accordance with the terms of the buy-sell agreements. Often, a life insurance policy provides funds for such an agreement.

If you have to handle the sale alone, you may find that the process is more difficult than selling other properties. Determining the value of a business is very complex. It is not just the piece of property, but the value of the business compared with other enterprises. You can hire professional appraisers to evaluate potential income, book value and market value, common stock of the company, liquidation value, historical rates of return, or price-earnings ratio. If you lack expertise in this area, you may want to hire a qualified specialist to negotiate the terms of sale. You may find that people are already interested in purchasing the business, including owners of similar businesses, partners, customers, and family members.

CHAPTER 14

Trust Investing

When your duties as trustee involve investing for the estate, it is essential that you establish an investment policy statement (IPS) no matter how small or large the estate. The policy statement forces you to examine investment objectives, risks, and constraints involved in investing. The written policy also provides you with a worksheet on how the markets are acting to keep estate investments in a secure and profitable position.

Investment Policy Statement

The IPS is not only a good idea for you as a trustee, but also as an informative tool for anyone working with and for the estate. Other professionals you employ will have a better understanding of how and why you are taking certain investment measures. The IPS provides a way to review investment performance and change investments if necessary. You can use the policy to rethink changes in tax or other laws and make long-term alterations. It also makes it easier for you to explain to beneficiaries why you are making certain investments, and, of course, you can use the IPS if any claims are filed against you so you can show the court why you took certain measures.

It is your responsibility to create this policy based on good information and recommendations from qualified investment counselors. You can enlist the help of a financial adviser in putting together a policy statement if you are inexperienced in creating one. Naturally, you should check into an adviser's background first. You may want to seek out an adviser who is not managing the investments to avoid any self-serving recommendations. The estate's size and complexities will determine the length and details of the policy statement. The IPS should include goals and objectives, time frames, risk acceptability, management, income needs, strategies for asset allocation, financial advisers, procedures for monitoring and evaluating advisers or managers, reviews, and amendments.

The creation and continued review of the IPS is often considered to be the fiduciary or trustee's most important duty. It will be the planning schedule and foundation you follow when dealing with all investments during estate administration. It also helps you make financial decisions. In the end, it helps you study returns, examine risk-taking, and eventually increase the probability of success for those investments. It will help you avoid panic during an ever-changing financial market, and will keep you from making spontaneous decisions when you become overconfident with investments. In short, the policy statement prevents you from making the day-to-day choices that often lead to short-term opportunities and keeps you focused on the long-term goals for the estate's investments. This is important when the market goes into temporary gains and slides that often trick investors in the end. A trustee who creates a satisfactory IPS becomes disciplined and knowledgeable, regardless of past experience. The plan will help you establish investment guidelines, focusing on appropriate moves and strategies in the marketplace instead of impulsive choices. Once you establish the policy, it is easier to follow a particular plan, allowing you to spend more time on other matters of the estate.

The policy statement mostly will remain the same throughout your tenure as trustee, but you may change it when shifts are necessary because of changing market trends. However, you will need to make these changes with the long-term investment goals in mind. An IPS also opens up better communication between you and the beneficiaries. It clarifies issues of importance and concern and deters misunderstanding. It leads to a better relationship with the beneficiaries, who will more than likely agree to the investment moves you are making.

A typical policy statement will be only a few pages. The introduction will explain the basics of the trust and will include essential information, such as the name and description of the trust, the beneficiaries, and what type of property and income are involved. It will describe the terms the grantor has established for you and for the beneficiaries. It will also include what happens to assets upon the grantor's death. It may include references to a durable power of attorney or appointments and steps to be taken when minor children are involved. The IPS should mention sources of authority, such as the trust document itself and state laws. It may add the amounts of trust assets in cash and securities. It should include details of current and future beneficiaries with information on their status as far as the trust document is concerned, including current and future income they are entitled to. The policy should explain your fees and expenses, based on instructions from the trust document.

Following the introduction, you may want to explain the objectives of the investment policy. You might point out that the reasons for the policy, including making investments prudently, producing moderate income without risk to the estate and beneficiaries, meeting periodic needs to use principal for market reasons that are appropriate for the beneficiaries, increasing the value of principal over time, and minimizing expenses for efficient investing. You may want to be more specific when it comes to monetary figures you need to maintain in regard to investing and preserving the grantor's standard of living. You can point out ways to minimize taxation for the investments. You can also describe policy goals, such as terms of time horizon, performance, risks, and asset allocations that include guidelines for cash equivalents, domestic fixed income, domestic equities, and international equities. You may want to devote a section to the selection of investment managers, basing such choices on historical performance, risk and reward measurements, investment strategies, familiarity with investing, structure of the portfolio, and circumstances that might lead you to reconsider guidelines as time goes on. You also might want to include a description of how you will monitor investment managers. You might explain when it would be a good time to make changes in the fund's organization or replace an adviser. You should explain evaluation and performance of investments, including how you will judge the investment while you are administering the estate.

Planning an IPS obviously takes much thought and consideration. However, you can liken it to talking to yourself, therefore making it easier to make decisions. More importantly, an IPS shows that you are sincerely involved in making the best investment decisions for the estate and its beneficiaries. You will be able to demonstrate that you are following a plan in the best interest of the estate.

CASE STUDY: MAP OUT YOUR GOALS

Philip G. Blumel, CFP
Raymond James & Associates, Inc.
515 N. Flagler Ave.
West Palm Beach, FL 33401
(561) 835-1040

Without an investor policy statement that clearly maps out the goals and parameters, you do not know where to go or how to get there. You cannot get lost with an IPS that guides every investment and decision.

Put together the IPS with a person in the legal business with whom you plan on working. That way, you can craft the IPS to best fit the particular situation, and both you and the investment manager or planner are familiar with the logic of each part of it. It is always a good idea to work with someone experienced in legal dealings every step of the way. The financial planner often takes a birds-eye view and can help manage the process.

The creation of an estate plan has to fit the special details of the situation, and every family's is different. Deciding who should — or who must — know what and when are details planners must take into account. There is no general rule.

As a trustee, you need everything to be explicit — goals, risk tolerance, and other parameters — and choose traditional and time-tested tools to achieve them. Then, monitor and review the plan over time. This framework is not innovative, exciting, or glamorous; it is simply good practice, for which you will enjoy the more fundamental rewards of confidence and respect.

Managing Investments

As trustee, you must manage all investments according to the needs of the beneficiaries, the trust agreement, and state or local laws. Depending on the trust document, you might have over-all power to manage investments, or you could be obligated to consult with professional advisers. A trust document can provide details about which stocks or funds you should invest in for the trust, or it could restrict investments in certain categories. Your investment responsibilities may differ, depending on whether you are making decisions for a terminating trust or for a continuing trust.

A terminating trust ends at the grantor's death. As with a personal representative, the trustee in this case must preserve assets and raise the cash needed to pay the necessary estate expenses, taxes, cash, bequests, and other financial matters. You should take action to prevent obvious losses from occurring. The stock market has ups and downs even the best experts cannot predict. However, when a certain stock begins to take a sudden tumble, it would be up to you to sell the stock and save what is left for the beneficiaries, or buy a more promising investment depending on your expertise or the advice of a knowledgeable stockbroker. The trustee handling a terminating trust is not necessarily responsible for making more money for the beneficiaries, but instead tries to keep the investments as safe and secure as possible.

A trustee managing a continuing trust has the ongoing job of watching the investments during the life of the trust. In most cases, you will invest in securities that maximize current income for the beneficiaries. A trustee for this type of trust must have expertise with investing or have a close relationship with an experienced investment adviser. You need to produce enough income to meet the financial needs of the beneficiaries, cover the expenses of the estate, and often invest in diversified stocks to hedge against inflation or other unexpected future changes to protect the interests of the remaindermen.

When making investments, you must always remember the duties of loyalty and impartiality to the beneficiaries. An investment portfolio's overall performance is not as important as the prudent way in which you invest. You can make both risky and conservative investments. It is not necessarily the performance of one stock that matters, but how well it works in bringing financial growth in the overall investment strategy. Of course, you should try to minimize risk and avoid improper investments, which would include investments you have a personal interest in, short-term investments that promise a fast profit, unproductive property, unsecured loans, and investments that diminish over time. Investing for the long term is what most financial planners would advise when handling investments. Investing in diversified stocks is a simple rule that can protect an investment portfolio if one or more stocks are disappointing. Mutual funds have become popular in recent years because they include this diversity of stocks.

If you do not feel confident in handling investments alone, you can seek the help of a financial adviser. However, this does not leave you free and clear from any investment actions. You are still responsible for all holdings. The Uniform Prudent Investor Act lets you delegate investment responsibility to an investment adviser, but the act still leaves you in charge overall. You are responsible for selecting a qualified financial agent and establishing the terms of investment procedures. Therefore, you must communicate with a financial manager on a regular basis. You should keep close watch over all stocks and bonds invested, making sure the amount of income meets trust expenses and the needs of the beneficiaries. Regardless of your expertise in investing or lack of it, selecting an investment adviser to at least assist in evaluating or managing the portfolio is a wise choice for a busy trustee.

You should review the portfolio periodically as markets and the needs of the beneficiaries change. Financial experts encourage trustees to review the portfolio at least once a year. Others say it should be done every few months. Reviewing investments allows you to measure how well the portfolio is doing and how much the investment manager has achieved based on the goals you set. If you need to change investments because of poor performance, you can make the proper adjustments. This is also true of switching financial advisers. If you feel the manager you selected has not performed up to your expectations, you should not hesitate to seek new advice.

Often, changes in the financial needs of beneficiaries may require adjustments to certain investments, switching them to stocks or funds that promise better performance. In general, financial advisers will explain that diversification in the portfolio is the best way to invest safely. This includes investing in various types of securities, such as stocks, bonds, cash, real estate, and mortgages. However, it is also important to invest across a wide range of industries, including technology, finance, utilities, and transportation.

Mutual Fund Investing 101

Simply put, mutual funds are just a means to invest in something along with many other people. The advantage you have in doing this, rather than investing your money individually in something, is that you will have a professional fund manager whose job is to look after the invested funds and make any necessary adjustments in light of his or her knowledge and experience. The mutual fund as a whole amounts to much more money than you could invest alone, which may open up possibilities for investment by the manager that can produce greater returns. The large size of the portfolio means that the manager can diversify the holdings much more than you could on your own, and this spreads the risk.

There are a wide range of potential purchases for the manager. It is not as simple as just buying some stocks or bonds; there are many variations available for the mutual fund manager to choose from, and you will select the fund and management according to both the level of risk that you find acceptable and your hoped-for return. You can invest in money market funds, income funds, growth funds, value funds, index funds, sector funds, international funds, and many other permutations. Successful investing takes considerable time, and you will find that, overall, the price you pay for professional management is relatively cheap compared with the value that you should be getting.

When you put money in a mutual fund, you become a shareholder in that fund just as if you had bought shares in a company on the stock market. The fund will usually have stated objectives for its investment plan, and this will cover things such as the type of shares or bonds that will be bought by the fund and how much risk the manager intends to take.

One of the best features of a mutual fund compared with investing individually is that a typical mutual fund controls a large amount of money. Because of this, the fund manager can buy stocks in many different companies, which gives the much-vaunted diversification that all the experts advise. Diversification ensures that any wrong stock pick will not have a marked effect on the value as a whole, even if that company should fail completely. There are so many companies represented in a typical fund that the fund is not affected much with a financial catastrophe at one of the companies, although it should be said that the manager will likely know enough to sell the shares before they reach that stage.

Which Investments?

Many books and software programs explain the best ways to safely put your money in a place where it will grow sufficiently over time. This is a comparatively brief summary on making money work for the trust:

- **Cash equivalents**: These investments include short-term certificates of deposit, money market funds, interest-bearing savings and checking accounts, and short-term U.S. Treasury bills. Some of these investments can be converted to cash quickly without loss of value. You would use them to meet short-term cash needs, such as taxes, fees, and anticipated distributions. You can place them in temporary holdings for more secure investments later on. Cash and cash equivalents are considered a safe way to invest. They are easy to handle, and you can transfer them with no difficulty. As trustee, you should have a reasonable amount on hand to use for immediate or unexpected payments. You should not use cash equivalents as long-term investments, as they would have a poor return. They do not have protection against inflation, and fluctuating interest rates make them undependable income. You must watch short-term investments at all times and be ready to transfer them for expenses or to stronger, more profitable investments.

- **Equities (stocks)**: These are ownership interests of common and preferred stockholders in a company. They are intended to produce high returns. Investors are rewarded with a greater appreciation of the company's stock as it grows. The broad categories for stocks include large-cap stocks from multibillion-dollar companies, mid-cap stocks from companies earning around $1 billion, and small-cap stocks, which are considered the riskiest because they tend to have volatile prices. Equities can produce some income for beneficiaries and help protect the overall portfolio from inflation. Although they are not completely without risk because of normal market fluctuations, equity investments perform well in most cases and are a reasonable way to keep the portfolio strong.

- **Bonds**: These marketable securities are considered good investments for a trust. They are often easily evaluated, and you can sell them quickly when you need cash immediately. Bonds include fixed income securities issued by corporations and through city, state, and federal governments. The interest paid is often higher than dividends from common stocks. Prices on the bond can drop, however, if market interest rates are higher than the price of a bond during the limited term of the bond obligation. The bond's price will be higher if the market rates are lower. A bond held to maturity will bring its full value to the investor.

- **Mutual funds**: These investments are popular with the average investor because of their diversity. Mutual funds pool money from stocks, bonds, money markets, and other investments. Unless the trust agreement says otherwise, state laws usually allow trustees to invest in them. As with all other investments, you should obtain written permission from the trust's beneficiaries to invest in mutual funds.

Bond Investing 101

The modern concept of a bond was developed during the early 1800s. England passed a new law allowing loans to become a negotiable instrument and establishing formal bond issues that stated how much was being borrowed, when the bonds would come due, and the terms under which the money was being borrowed. Subsequent issues of the same bond followed the same terms, and bonds were issued in large amounts to satisfy the needs of large-scale investors.

A bond is issued when a federal or state government, municipality, or corporation decides that a bond is the most appropriate way to raise the funds needed for a particular purpose or project. These decisions are made with the assistance of a financial advisor or a consultant. The federal government and federal agencies use the services of internal financial advisors. Municipalities and local governments, who issue bonds only occasionally, characteristically hire outside consultants to work with their finance directors and legal staff in collecting all the necessary documentation and statistical information. Corporations rely on the services of their investment banks.

A government or municipality issues bonds to raise money for public undertakings, expecting to repay the debt using tax revenues or, in the case of a revenue-generating project, such as a toll road or a university dormitory, from future income when the project is completed. A corporation may choose to issue a bond to finance an expansion of its operations or the acquisition of another business, expecting to repay the debt from the future income generated by its increased business activity.

The preparation of a bond issue is a highly orchestrated process requiring the participation of several legal and financial entities. Once it has been established that a bond issue is appropriate and a preliminary draft has been prepared, the contract (bond indenture) is reviewed by a bond counsel who gives a legal opinion. The bond counsel determines whether the bond issue is appropriate for the debt being incurred, the legal position of the bondholders relative to other creditors, and the tax status of the interest paid by the bond.

During the preparation of the bond indenture, the issuer must decide whether to include a call provision and whether the bond issue will be paid off in increments or all at once. A call option gives the bond issuer the right to redeem the bond issue before its maturity date, more often than not when interest rates fall. Many bond issues have fixed call options, allowing the issuer to redeem the bond only after a certain period of time has elapsed. A municipal bond may have a call provision triggered when specific circumstances arise. A single issue consisting of bonds with different maturity dates is called a serial bond. A term bond is one with a fixed, long-term maturity date. Many U.S. government and corporate bonds are term bonds.

A bond may have a senior lien, meaning that if the bond issuer declares bankruptcy, bond holders will be given priority over other creditors when cash is distributed. A holder of a bond with a junior lien will be placed in a subordinate position to other creditors.

Types of bonds

United States Treasury and Agency bonds currently make up the largest segment of the U.S. bond market. Treasury bonds are backed by the full faith and credit of the U.S. government. The U.S. Treasury issues a variety of bond types, including Treasury bills, Treasury notes, Treasury bonds, Treasury Inflation Protection Securities (TIPS), and savings bonds.

Agency bonds are issued by federal government agencies, such as the Federal Home Loan Mortgage Corporation (Freddie Mac), Federal National Mortgage Corporation (Fannie Mae), and the Small Business Administration (SBA). They are not backed by the full faith and credit of the U.S. government, but are given the highest credit ratings because they are associated with the federal government and are considered to be fundamental to its operation. Agency bonds make up about 18 percent of the bonds held by individual households.

Corporate bonds are issued by corporations to raise financing for a variety of purposes, including expansion, the purchase of new equipment, and company acquisitions. Corporate bonds are rated according to the credit worthiness of the companies that issue them. Because corporations have a higher potential of default than a municipality, agency, or the U.S. government, they tend to have lower ratings and pay a higher yield. Having said this, there are corporations rated in the highest rating category — General Electric being one of them.

Municipal bonds are issued by counties, townships, cities, schools, or tax districts to finance public projects, such as roads, bridges, stadiums, or sewage treatment plants. Municipal bonds fall into two categories: revenue bonds and general obligation bonds. Revenue bonds repay investors out of the revenues generated by the completion of the property, such as the tolls collected from a toll road. General obligation bonds are guaranteed by the taxing authority that is issuing the bonds. Interest paid by municipal bonds is generally, but not always, tax exempt, making them particularly attractive to investors in higher income tax brackets.

Zero coupon bonds are sold to investors at a deep discount to the bond's face value. They pay no regular interest, but the investor is paid the face value of the bond at maturity. The difference between the discounted price and the face value equals the interest paid on the principal.

Mortgage-backed bonds are secured by deeds to real estate, equipment, or other hard assets. The mortgages are normally residential, but they can be commercial in some cases.

International bonds are debt instruments issued by other countries. International bonds are subject to additional risks, such as sovereign risk and currency risk.

Bond mutual funds pool together investor capital to purchase individual bond securities. Bond mutual funds are managed by a professional portfolio manager, and can have a variety of objectives related to risk, industry sectors, international investment, and length of maturity. Bond funds offer investors flexibility and diversification. They do not have a maturity date because bonds are replaced with new bond purchases as they mature. Bond funds incur management fees and may charge a load fee or an exit fee. Bond ETFs are investment pools similar to bond mutual funds, but are sold as shares on the stock market and can be traded throughout the day like stocks.

Explaining investment strategy and conditions

As explained in Chapter 8, the estate's personal representative and trustee should have an initial meeting with beneficiaries to explain the plans and provisions of a will and trust, become acquainted with each other, and define what the beneficiaries have to look forward to in the future. Follow-up meetings from time to time may be appropriate.

One key factor in communicating with beneficiaries is the prepared investment policy statement. This is something you should discuss with the beneficiaries as soon as it is ready and convenient for all sides. Although many trustees do not bother to get beneficiaries involved in the financial planning statement, doing so lets everyone involved know you are sincere and careful when it comes to investing income from the estate. It lets the beneficiaries know your intentions and reassures them of your care amid an uncertain financial market. You do not have to explain every detail in the policy statement, however, because it is more geared to you.

When you get to know the beneficiaries' personalities, you can then decide how best to explain the investment plans. Sometimes a simple letter helps out. In the letter, you might explain a shorter version of the policy statement, pointing out the reasons for managing certain investments and the long-term objectives that will be in the best interests of the estate and the beneficiaries. The letter could be similar to the policy statement itself, but discussed more briefly. You could explain the sources of authority, purposes of the trust, current considerations, investment objectives, performance, and asset selection.

You are not required to prepare projections for beneficiaries, but keeping them informed in all affairs, including investments, is a legal obligation. You should make projections for owner benefit in handling the estate. That is a main reason for the investment policy statement. You need to know the market conditions affecting investments to keep the estate in stable shape. If a beneficiary demands to receive projections and you do not want to spend valuable time on this effort, you could hand the task over to a financial adviser at the beneficiary's expense, or you could possibly claim it as an expense of the trust if the trust agreement permits this.

Beneficiaries may not necessarily be knowledgeable about the facts surrounding the stock market. Projections are merely intelligent estimates as to where stocks may be going, but they are by no means always accurate. Presenting them with high hopes may only lead to disappointment later on if the investments underperform. You should inform beneficiaries of this and tell them that you are making the investments with their best interest in mind, but projections are not a certainty.

You might present long-term projections when looking at investments and trends for future years. These projections help beneficiaries understand that investing money in one area would be beneficial to them in the end, in which case they could then have the financial protection or funds of greater value at a later date. Usually, the longer a projection is, the greater its value will be down the road because of compounded interest. You may occasionally make short-term projections and investments because of a beneficiary's changing lifestyles. This might make it necessary to move the investment to another place to gain the necessary profits that can help the beneficiary. These are usually detailed projections because they deal with specific assets.

Investment statements, although done for your benefit to keep track of trends, are also a good way to communicate with beneficiaries. Most experts believe trustees should report financial activity to the beneficiaries on a regular basis to avoid any unnecessary anxiety or suspicion by the beneficiaries. Quarterly statements are suggested for small estates, but you could also provide them monthly because banks and creditors usually provide monthly statements to customers. A monthly statement is especially recommended when the portfolio is very active. Explain to beneficiaries how to read a statement if you think they lack the expertise. Explain the difference between income and principal, carrying costs, fee calculations, and reasons for fluctuations in income in each statement. You could offer the statements online to beneficiaries who have access to a computer.

It is a sad fact that stocks can take a big hit in a changing market, regardless of the investor's intentions and knowledge. You may have to explain this to beneficiaries when an investment experiences a sudden loss. Of course, investors sometimes make bad decisions, resulting in losses. That is the reason for diversified investing, in which the investor has a variety of holdings in different financial areas, offsetting any downward trends in certain markets. Market crashes can also occur, causing widespread losses in all investments. Although most stocks usually recover, it can take time.

When a sudden loss does occur, explain it to the beneficiaries, regardless of how difficult it may be. Hoping that the beneficiaries will not notice and that the stock will soon rise again is wishful thinking. Some beneficiaries do pay attention to the market, and even those who do not may get upset upon learning about an investment failure without being notified by you. When bad news happens, it is best for you to contact the beneficiaries immediately and let them know all the facts. Explain the nature of the problem and the reasons they should not be alarmed. The stock may pick up, or you might sell it in favor of a healthier investment to regain any money lost. If you invest wisely and diversify, it is almost a certainty that most stocks in the trust's portfolio will regain their original strength and go on to make more financial gains. You should tell the beneficiaries what happened and what you are doing to remedy the problem as soon as possible. At any rate, it is better that the beneficiary learns about a problem from you directly rather than see it on an investment statement. Even if your mistake caused the loss, it is best to own up to it to show your honesty and forthrightness. Explain the error and inform the beneficiaries how it will be corrected. It is a possibility that you can be sued for such events.

If you suspect that a beneficiary may be rash and seek court action too soon, you may want to consult an attorney before engaging in discussions with the beneficiary. The attorney could assure you that you acted within the boundaries of your authority and that documentation will show all decisions were prudent and done in the best interest of the beneficiary. In some cases, an attorney may have to make suggestions for a settlement. This is where proper documents and insurance policies come in handy for you. Taking all matters into consideration early on will be of enormous help during the administration of the estate.

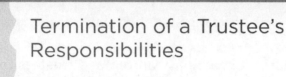
Termination of a Trustee's
Responsibilities

T he trustee may resign, be removed, or have his or her duties
end because of death, loss of capacity, or the normal termination of the trust.

When a Trustee is Relieved of Duties

You usually will be able to resign your duties as trustee if the
trust agreement allows it. Resignation is also possible with the
approval of the beneficiaries, as long as the agreement allows
them to grant permission. You would have to petition the court
for permission to resign in all other instances. You should have
no difficulty getting permission to resign as long as the trust is
in good order and your resignation will not have a detrimental effect. Courts normally do not want a trust to be handled by
someone who is reluctant to continue. Therefore, you should take
the time to explain that staying on would be a burden to you
and would not be in the best interest of the estate. Many trustees
are forced to resign because of failing health or an unexpected

increase in personal responsibility. You may find it to be a disadvantage financially to continue your duties. Regardless of the reason, you should be able to show the court why it is no longer possible for you to continue in the position. Notify all beneficiaries of your resignation, according to directions provided in the trust document or by the court. You should give notice as soon as possible before your official resignation date.

Certain beneficiaries or persons can remove trustees from their duties if authorized by the trust agreement. A trust protector might have been appointed and can ask for your resignation without giving reasons for it. Trustees are often relieved of their duties because they become incapacitated. The court may remove you if it finds your continued administration would be detrimental to the trust. Trustees have also been removed for committing serious breaches of trust or crimes. Removal may be requested because of favoritism toward one beneficiary over another, being uncooperative with a co-trustee or another professional, or fraud. Sometimes, friction between you and the beneficiaries can lead them to call for a resignation. However, they need sufficient proof to show you are detrimental to the trust and would not serve the beneficiaries' best interests if continuing in the job. If you find yourself in financial difficulty, the court could remove you if it learns of the situation and determines that it would be unhealthy to the trust if you continue handling the estate. Courts are usually more reluctant to relieve the duties of a trustee named by a grantor than one appointed by the court. However, it depends on the severity of the situation and how much it affects the court.

If you die or lose the capacity to manage the trust, the trust property would pass on to a surviving co-trustee or a named successor. In other cases, state laws and courts usually determine the replacement. You might want to prepare a memorandum to provide information on the trust for a possible succeeding trustee in case of future unexpected consequences. Obviously, it is not necessary to operate a trust as if an unexpected event will occur. However, keeping information available is a good insurance policy for the trust if such an event should happen.

Other situations

If you have not been removed, but are simply preparing to end your duties of administering the trust, you have certain responsibilities to follow before officially resigning. You should identify the successor trustee and have written proof of the new trustee's acceptance. You cannot and should not transfer duties to a successor before your resignation is effective. You should not make any transfers until the resignation is executed by the appropriate parties, beneficiaries, or the court, depending on the situation. You should be able to account for all administrative procedures until the intended day of resignation. You should give the succeeding trustee a copy of your resignation, all data concerning the beneficiaries, a tax log for the current year, copies of tax returns for the past three years, a list of assets with tax costs, the original trust agreement, and copies of the trust accounting. The successor should give you transfer instructions for the assets, receipts for assets transferred, receipts of all documents, and a copy of the appointment and acceptance of the successor trustee.

The trust may terminate on its own over a period of time. A trust's period eventually expires, and you can distribute assets. A grantor could revoke a trust if this right was reserved in the establishment of the trust. A trust can be revoked during a grantor's lifetime, or even after death by direction of the will in some cases. The grantor must usually give you notice of termination and notify beneficiaries. If the trust agreement does not contain a stated power to revoke the trust, it cannot be revoked. In some cases, you may be asked to consent to having the trust revoked. You would review your responsibilities to the trust before consenting. When an attempt is made to revoke a trust, it is your duty to make sure any revocation is proper before agreeing to assist in revoking the trust. You may have to use legal means to try to block a revocation if you deem the action to be improper.

The trust could also be terminated if terms of the trust document no longer exist. For example, the trust may be set up for a beneficiary until that beneficiary receives a certain amount of income. Once the beneficiary receives that amount, the trust would be terminated.

A trust can be rescinded when it is learned it should not have been created. This action is quite common. It can happen if the grantor created the trust by mistake, undue influence, duress, or fraud. Trustees or potential trustees should take note if they believe a grantor has been misled about the advantages of creating a trust. The grantor may be easily influenced, mentally incompetent, or caving to pressure from self-serving relatives or unscrupulous salespeople.

Emergency situations might also terminate your responsibilities as trustee. There may be a money-losing proposition in operating a business under the trust. In such a case, a court might authorize the sale of the business and distribution of the proceeds to save the trust money before the business's value declines. Other reasons where it becomes impractical for you to continue as trustee can lead to termination, as well as when you could cause financial harm to the trust.

The beneficiaries could decide to terminate the trust when it is no longer necessary to carry out the purpose of the trust. To do this, you would have to obtain consent from each beneficiary. You also must make an effort to make sure no beneficiary is incapacitated or no undue influence is involved. A beneficiary can always withdraw a consent in such situations. In that case, the other beneficiaries cannot bring about termination of the trust.

The Trustee's Responsibilities

You must make distributions, transfers, and titles of the trust property as soon as possible when a termination is in order. You should be careful with all actions you take. Even though it is important to finish your trust duties, you must make all distributions in accordance with the trust instructions. You remain in your position until the trust is terminated, and even afterward if certain duties are required.

You must ascertain the correct identities of all parties. This if often easy if the beneficiaries are direct descendants of the grantor. However, it can sometimes be difficult, especially if a large family is involved and deaths have occurred. It can be challenging work, but you must be certain to identify all beneficiaries and do the legwork it takes to make distributions according to the trust. It can be even more difficult when children of the beneficiaries are to receive distributions at a certain time or age. You must verify all information before termination of the trust. It is a good idea for you to periodically update information on the beneficiaries, such as addresses or changes in family members, during the term of administration.

Sometimes, you will have advance notice that the trust will be terminated soon. This is a good time to get all accounting information in order and notify beneficiaries when they are likely to receive distributions, what the approximate expenses may be, and what shares they have coming to them. The trust itself may actually continue to exist for an additional period, allowing you to finish up with the trust's affairs. In this case, the trust would exist as a separate taxable entity, and titles to some of the trust's property may remain with you for the time being until you complete a full accounting and distributions. You should make all distributions within a reasonable time.

When you have distributed all trust assets, you should submit a final accounting to all beneficiaries for their approval. You may require the beneficiaries to approve the accounting in writing and perhaps sign release forms absolving you of any further liability. When you make the last distributions to the beneficiaries, you would file a final tax return.

Tax Consequences and Accounting

The trust is an entity that is taxable until you have distributed all trust property to the beneficiaries. It is also taxable during a reasonable time afterward, in which it is necessary for you to complete those distributions. When the trust is legally terminated, the gross income, credits, and deductions of the trust now belong to the beneficiaries for tax purposes.

You must report all income of the trust as distributed to the beneficiaries in the final year of the trust. Net operating losses, deductions, capital losses, and carry-overs become available to the beneficiary succeeding to the distributions of the property. Sometimes, you will not be able to distribute income immediately because you may need to retain money pending exact amounts that you will distribute. This temporary withholding of funds should not affect the normal tax treatment.

Tax accounting differs from trust accounting because it determines the tax costs to the trust and the beneficiaries. Trust accounting is used to determine the calculations of income and principal distributed to the beneficiaries.

As trustee and legal owner of the trust, you must spell out principal and income for accounting purposes in accordance with the federal Uniform Principal and Income Act. This act concerns how income is earned during the settlement of an estate and how it is to be distributed, when income interest begins in the trust, what property is principal and will go to beneficiaries, who receives it, and how trust receipts and disbursements should be allocated between principal and income. You need to know which distributions are income and which are principal. You need to know if the estate has received the proper amounts in principal and income, or if beneficiaries have made payments that would cause a reduction in distribution that would lead to a reduction in tax deductions. The beneficiaries are entitled to net income when income interest begins, according to a date specified in the trust, or when an asset becomes subject to the trust. When income interest ends, you should pay to the beneficiaries any undistributed income received before the termination of the interest.

Allocation of receipts to principal includes receipts from corporations, partnerships, common trust funds, real estate investment trusts, investment companies, and other organizations that specialize in business and activities. Property other than money, money received in exchange for a trust's interest, money received from liquidation, and money received from an investment company are allocated to principal.

Some other receipts allocated to principal include:

- Amounts recovered from third parties to reimburse the trust

- Proceeds of property taken by eminent domain

- Net income received in an accounting period not yet distributed

- Amounts held subject to the terms of a lease

- Proceeds from the sale or disposition of any obligation to be paid to the trustee

- Proceeds of life insurance policies

- Proceeds from the sale of non-income-producing property

- Proceeds from the granting of options or gains

- Amounts received as distributions of principal from a trust or an estate

Some receipts allocated to income include:

- Receipts from entities in the form of money

- Proceeds of property taken by eminent domain constituting a separate award for loss of income

- Amounts received as rent of real or personal property

- Amounts received as distributions of income from a trust or estate

- Receipts from principal

Receipts usually apportioned between principal and income include deferred compensation, annuities, and similar payments. Certain assets, including patents, royalty rights, and lottery prizes, lose value over a limited time. You must allocate 10 percent of the payments from these assets to income and the balance to principal. Receipts from interest in natural resources can be income and principal. Receipts from asset-backed securities are income. Allocations that are insubstantial are usually allocated to principal. Your compensation is typically split evenly between income and principal.

Accounting should include a summary that reveals the level of detail, such as assets from the beginning of the term, transactions during the period, and the assets at the end of the period. Transactions during the period of the trust may include the total dividends and interest received on each security. You must also disclose your commissions and fees. Detail distributions to the beneficiaries to include bequests, distributions of income, and distributions of principal. You should include details of payments to creditors, other payments, funeral expenses, and administrative expenses. You should disclose purchases made during the administration of the trust.

When receiving a trust accounting as a successor trustee or beneficiary, here are some important features to consider:

- The total of trustee commissions and fees paid, as well as how they were calculated

- That all provisions have complied with the trust agreement and local laws

- The accuracies of numbers and details agree with summary reports

- The trustee's responsibilities in handling all losses incurred

- All administrative expenses are reasonable

You should store records retained permanently or for a certain number of years when termination of the trust has been completed. The choice of using physical space or having records on computer files is up to you and your own expense. Eventually, you may receive inquiries from beneficiaries or representatives about verification of distributions. Accurate records will make it easier for you to provide information that is helpful to people with questions about assets, even if it is not your job at that time. Tax authorities may also make inquiries about information needed for tax purposes. Overall, however, your job as trustee is now completed.

CHAPTER 16

A Sampling of Trusts

A trust can be established during the lifetime of the grantor and can survive the grantor's death. A trust can even be formed after the grantor's death, if the will instructs it. All trusts remain under the rules and instructions of the trust agreement. All assets belong to the trust itself and not to the trustee, who is administering the trust. To better perform your duties as trustee, you should become knowledgeable about the many types of trusts available. Beneficiaries, relatives, and friends may also benefit from understanding the different types of trusts. Even though all trusts can be divided into two basic categories — revocable and irrevocable — various trust types within those categories are more detailed and specified for the beneficiaries. The following trusts are just a sampling of the many types available.

Revocable and Irrevocable Trusts

Living trusts can be revocable or irrevocable. The grantor may modify the terms or cancel a revocable living trust. When the trust is revoked, the grantor resumes ownership of the trust property. In some cases and under particular circumstances, living trusts allow income to be taxed to a beneficiary, while providing income-tax savings to the grantor. However, income earned through an established trust for a beneficiary under the age of 14 may be taxed at the same tax rate as the beneficiary's parents. Transferring property to a living trust may also be subject to a gift tax.

Revocable living trusts are set up during the grantor's lifetime. The grantor owns the assets during his or her life. The assets, which the beneficiaries will receive at the grantor's death, will be held in the trust, which means taking the estate through probate is not necessary. The trustee handles the trust in the same way an executor handles a will. The trust is created primarily for tax purposes. It can be altered, amended, or terminated at any time during the grantor's life.

The revocable living trust is one of the most widely used estate-planning instruments, and is a top choice for many grantors in selecting an administrative plan because it addresses several concerns.

First, it is a way to avoid probate for many people. Property held in this particular trust does not have to go through the court-supervised process after the grantor's death. Only property owned by an individual goes through probate. The title of the property held in a trust is registered in the name of the trust, and therefore the estate is spared the cost and time-consuming process of probate court.

A revocable living trust also minimizes or eliminates federal taxes. The federal estate tax can be the largest expense triggered by a person's death. However, a revocable living trust, as long as it is properly prepared, includes provisions that exempt a husband and wife from any such taxes, making sure the property can pass swiftly to family members and other beneficiaries.

The trust also protects the grantor during times of incapacity. Whether the person becomes mentally or physically incapacitated, a durable power of attorney or trust can handle the grantor's financial affairs. This avoids the expense and uncertainty of a court-appointed guardian in cases where an incapacitated person does not have planned protection.

Another protective measure is that the incapacitated grantor's affairs are a matter of public record because the court supervises all proceedings in handling financial matters. Permission for payments made on the grantor's behalf must be obtained from the court. The living trust is much stronger than a durable power of attorney in this regard because financial institutions, which have some limitations on monetary concerns, are open to orders of the court. The trustee has the power to handle the estate of the incapacitated grantor until that person is no longer incapacitated either because of recovery or death.

A revocable trust does not have an asset-protection advantage. During the grantor's lifetime, assets are moved to the trust and remain available to creditors. The trust makes it more difficult for creditors to access the assets, however, because creditors must petition for a court order that allows them to get to the assets held in the trust. The revocable trust usually evolves into an irrevocable trust at the grantor's death.

A revocable trust is typically set up when the grantor does not want to lose control of the trust property permanently, does not know how well-managed the trust will be in the hands of the trustee, or is uncertain of the proper duration for the trust. A revocable trust allows some assets in the trust to accept deposits or withdrawals during the grantor's lifetime. It also allows the grantor to change the trust's terms and the manner in which it is administered. The grantor can make the trust irrevocable at any time in the future. Assets from the trust are usually taxable, but grantors may choose this type of trust to avoid probate.

With an irrevocable trust, no one can take property away from the trust. Even the grantor cannot take property out of the trust. The trust cannot be altered, changed, modified in any way, or revoked after its creation. This type of trust is designed to minimize estate and income taxes. The trustee for an irrevocable trust can act more independently because each type of trust is unique. Grantors may choose such a trust because income from irrevocable trusts may not be taxable to the grantor, and because assets from the trust may not be subject to estate taxes. These benefits will be lost, however, if the grantor is entitled to receive income, use the trust assets, or control the administration of the trust in any way inconsistent with tax codes.

The grantor may purchase survivorship life insurance, which an irrevocable trust can hold and use for estate tax planning purposes, usually in large estates. An irrevocable life insurance trust is often used to benefit a spouse, children, or other heirs. It holds insurance on the grantor's life to benefit family members, and it protects the insurance proceeds from creditors, estate tax, and whomever a spouse might marry after the grantor's death.

Irrevocable Life Insurance Trusts

This is an important trust because many people do not understand that insurance is not necessarily tax-free outside of an insurance trust. Life insurance is taxable in the estate if the grantor owns the policy. Life insurance may escape taxation if paid to a spouse, but up to 50 percent of insurance proceeds could be paid later in estate taxes upon the spouse's death. Setting up a life insurance trust can avoid estate taxes and protect the financial future of family members. Most trusts can hold insurance policies and receive insurance proceeds, but life insurance trusts are created to insure the grantor and other family members.

Under an irrevocable life insurance trust, the ownership of life insurance is removed from the grantor and avoids taxation of the policy at the grantor's death. The grantor may deposit funds to the trust periodically that cover any payments of premiums or administration costs. The trustee should be aware that the grantor must survive three years in order to avoid having proceeds taxed when an insurance policy is transferred or added to the trust. The trustee is charged with notifying beneficiaries that they have a right to withdraw funds made to cover premiums and administrative costs. The trustee should check with the insurance agent on a periodic basis to be certain the policies are performing as expected.

Testamentary Trusts

Testamentary trusts must conform to the statutes that govern wills, as they are created as part of a will. The assets owned in the grantor's name are passed into the trust. This helps reduce the number of documents because the will and trust are in one document. This trust is also designed to minimize taxes and protect beneficiaries after the grantor's death. Testamentary trusts are frequently used to conserve or transfer wealth. The trustee is charged with administering the property in the trust and makes distributions to beneficiaries in accordance with trust provisions.

The estate is probated under a testamentary trust. The trust's assets are also subject to probate. The assets form the main portion of a testamentary trust and are often subject to generation-skipping transfer tax once the deceased person has died.

The grantor has substantial control over estate distribution in a testamentary trust. The trust also can help achieve significant savings in the future. For instance, it can provide for a child's education by delaying receipt of property until the child reaches the age of maturity. The estate also could escape estate taxation upon the death of a beneficiary later in life. The generation-skipping transfer tax, however, still may apply.

Marital Deduction Trusts

A grantor's spouse may benefit from several types of trusts. A revocable living trust can protect the spouse in the event of illness or disability. A grantor could also choose to use an irrevocable life insurance trust. It holds insurance on the grantor's life to benefit the spouse and children. The trust also protects insurance proceeds from creditors and estate tax.

Such trusts can be complicated and costly, but they ensure more control for the grantor. These trusts provide a number of tax benefits because of marital deductions. Every spouse is given the right to demand a specified minimum percentage of a deceased spouse's estate, as stipulated by state law. The surviving spouse may have the right to take a share of one-third of the assets. Alimony trusts can be used to fund alimony payments. This is typically done to minimize contact and interaction between the spouses.

A number of trusts qualify for a marital deduction for the surviving spouse. The trusts are the exclusive benefit of the survivor, so the trust is acting on behalf of only one beneficiary during the survivor's lifetime. Assets not disposed of will continue in the trust for others. Trust assets at the time of the surviving spouse's death are taxed as part of that spouse's estate. The grantor obtains a federal estate tax marital deduction for assets transferred to the trust. Assets donated during the grantor's life qualify for the federal gift-tax marital deduction.

The Qualified Terminable Interest Property (QTIP) Trust works for couples who do not share the same objectives for the disposition of estates. They want the surviving spouse to live comfortably, but want his or her own descendents (in second marriage situations, for example) to receive certain estate assets. The grantor of a QTIP trust can control where certain assets go at the surviving spouse's death, and can also obtain a marital deduction for his or her own estate.

Children's Trusts

These types of trusts may be the best option for many children, grandchildren, and other non-adult heirs. The trustee handles them until the child reaches the age of maturity. The trusts may provide important financial needs for education and care. Just about any trust can be used to benefit children or grandchildren. Children are usually the remainder beneficiaries, receiving assets after a preceding beneficiary's interests end.

The income-only minor's trust distributes all income annually to a grantor's child. It permits the grantor to make a gift of up to $13,000 per year, as well as qualify for annual gift-tax exclusion. The child is taxed on income earned by the trust. Under a special trust for children under age 21, the grantor can transfer $13,000 per year to the trust, which can accumulate income and qualify the grantor for an annual gift-tax exclusion. The child is not required to take assets by the age of 21, but has the right to do so.

Special needs trusts can be set up to benefit children with mental or physical ailments. These trusts restrict distributions to safeguard assets for the child's needs that the government and other services do not provide. Life insurance trusts also can benefit children with special needs.

Special Needs Trust

A special needs trust is established for people who receive government benefits to make certain the beneficiary is not disqualified from receiving such benefits. These trusts are legally permitted under the rules of social security, as long as a disabled beneficiary does not control the quantity or frequency of the trust distributions and cannot retract the trust. Often, people receiving government benefits can have their eligibility for such benefits reduced or eliminated through an inheritance or receipt of a gift. The special needs trust provides for luxuries or other benefits that the beneficiary normally would not get. The trust has a provision that terminates it if it could disqualify the beneficiary from government benefits.

The trust contains legal specifications that will maintain the comfort and happiness of disabled people in cases where they cannot be provided for through a private or public agency. Benefits can include medical and dental expenses, rehabilitation, treatment, insurance, essential dietary needs, education, and other services that help a special needs person function properly in society. Parents can set up a special needs trust in their general estate plan. Disabled people can also set up such trusts as long as someone else is named as the trustee.

Charitable Remainder Trusts

By donating assets to a charity, people receive a charitable-contribution tax deduction. The savings allow the grantor to invest in worthy charities, while minimizing income, federal gift, or estate taxes.

Charitable trusts may benefit a specific charity or the general public. The trusts are usually established as part of an estate plan to lower or avoid estate and gift tax. A charitable remainder trust (CRT) can be a financial planning tool if created during the lifetime of the grantor. The grantor can receive valuable lifetime financial benefits, and has the honor of being recognized by the charity he or she is helping.

The CRT must be irrevocable. Payments from the CRT must be for a term specified in years, not exceeding 20 years, or for the lives of beneficiaries in the trust. The yearly payment percentage should be equal to at least 5 percent of the fair market value of the assets in the trust, and it cannot have a payout of greater than 50 percent.

A charitable remainder annuity trust (CRAT) provides a fixed annuity for the grantor or beneficiaries designated in the trust agreement. The minimum rate of return to the beneficiaries must be a fixed amount and cannot be less than 5 percent. No further contributions can be made to it once the trust is established. A charitable remainder unitrust (CRUT) provides a variable-annuity benefit to beneficiaries. The minimum rate of return is also 5 percent.

A charitable lead trust (CLT) is set up to include deferring and controlling when heirs receive their funds, encouraging philanthropy and reducing gift- or estate-tax costs. The remainder beneficiaries wait to receive the property until the charitable beneficiary's interest expires. Charitable lead trusts have variations, just as charitable remainder trusts do. A charitable lead trust can be formed while the grantor is alive or according to instructions from the will. The earnings in a CLT are not taxed to the grantor, who will not receive an income-tax deduction for any charitable contributions during its term. However, the CLT can be structured as a grantor trust, in which the grantor is taxed on the income earned by the trust. The grantor will qualify for deduction for the charitable contributions made by the charitable lead trust. Establishing a CLT allows the grantor to have long-term charitable objectives, while coordinating with estate and financial planning to make certain that assets are available to children and other beneficiaries during the term.

Asset Protection Trust

Many asset protection trusts are unique in that they are created to protect a person's assets from claims by creditors in the future. The trusts are frequently set up in foreign countries. The assets do not always have to be transferred to countries outside the United States. When the asset protection trust is established, it insulates assets from any creditor attack. The trusts are usually designed to be an irrevocable form for a specified number of years and structured so the grantor is not a current beneficiary. The trust's undistributed assets are usually designed to return to the grantor upon termination of the trust, but only if there is no risk of creditor interference. The trust permits the grantor to regain complete control over the once-protected assets in the trust.

Trusts can protect assets in other ways, however. Defective trusts are irrevocable and provide asset protection benefits. They are treated as incomplete gifts for income-tax purposes to avoid income-tax procedures. Children's trusts have asset-protection motives by saving for the grantor's child, while also protecting valuable assets from a young child. Grantor retained annuity trusts (GRAT) are usually created to achieve tax savings when making large gifts. They provide asset protection for the principal. Proceeds from life insurance trusts are often protected.

Beneficiaries can benefit, while creditors are limited in their access to the proceeds.

Constructive Trust

Constructive trusts are implied trusts established by the courts, based on certain circumstances of the property held. Courts may decide the property owner had an intention to use the property for a certain person. Even though there was no formal declaration of a trust, the court may determine intentions of the deceased person, provided there is evidence of those intentions. In this complicated procedure, a person may have legal title to the property, but considerations are sometimes made for the possibility that the property actually belongs to someone else after the court weighs the facts.

Spendthrift Trust

Spendthrift provisions are sometimes included in a trust. They prevent a beneficiary from allowing a third party to be a party of interest to the trust. A spendthrift trust is established for the beneficiary so he or she will not sell or pledge away interests from the trust. Such trusts are protected from the beneficiaries' creditors until the trust property is eventually administered out of the trust and given to all recipients.

Tax Bypass Trust

Trusts that let one spouse leave money to the other, while limiting the amount of federal estate-tax payable on the death of the second spouse are called tax bypass trusts. Often, assets can pass on tax-free to a spouse, but when the surviving spouse dies the remaining assets would be taxable to the couple's children over and above the exempt limit. That can potentially be at a rate of 55 percent. The tax bypass trust avoids situations like this and, depending on the size and value of the estate, can save children hundreds of thousands of dollars in federal taxes.

Totten Trust

This type of trust is constructed when the grantor is still living. It gets its name from a 1904 court case in which the Court of Appeals of New York established the legality of this type of trust. The grantor deposits money into an account at a banking institution in the name of the grantor as a trustee for someone else. It is a type of revocable trust that is created so the gift is not completed until the grantor dies or becomes incapacitated during his or her lifetime. Any entity or person can be named as the recipient in the trust. Totten trust assets are able to avoid probate once the creator dies. The trust is mainly used with accounts and securities in financial institutions that include savings and bank accounts, as well as certificates of deposit. Totten trusts cannot be used with any real property. The trusts provide for a more secure way to pass assets to family members than by using joint ownership. It has been called a "poor man's" trust because a written trust document is usually not involved, and it often costs nothing for the grantor to establish.

CONCLUSION

When a loved one dies, we want to know that their final wishes were carried out as they had hoped. Being entrusted to carry out these wishes is an enormous responsibility, one that is dictated by specific laws that vary from state to state. Working with an attorney to ensure you settle the estate in accordance with these laws is necessary, especially if you have little experience dealing with taxes.

Settling a loved one's estate can be a taxing experience when trying to cope with his or her passing, especially if the area of estates is foreign to you. We hope this book has helped make the complex area of estate management clearer to you during this time.

The sample forms in Appendix A are provided to help you become acquainted with the various forms you will encounter upon being named executor. Remember that these forms vary from state to state, so contact the attorney assisting with your estate to find out about forms specific to your state. Following Appendix A, an extensive glossary is provided to answer any lingering questions you might have about terms that have been presented in the book.

APPENDIX

Sample Forms

The following forms are included to assist you in recognizing the forms often included in an estate. Some of the forms included in this book are state-specific and are only included as examples. You should use the forms specific to the state in which you live.

General Power of Attorney

BY THIS DOCUMENT, IT IS HEREBY ACKNOWLEDGED that I, **[name of person granting power of attorney]**, residing at **[street address]**, **[city]**, **[state/province]** **[zip/postal code]**, the undersigned, do hereby appoint **[name of person granted power of attorney]** of **[street address]**, **[city]**, **[state/province]** **[zip/postal code]** as my attorney-in-fact ("Agent") to exercise the powers and discretions described below.

If the Agent is unable to serve for any reason, I appoint [**alternate attorney-in-fact**], of [**street address**], [**city**], [**state/province**] [**zip/postal code**], as my alternate or successory Agent, as the case may be to serve with the same powers and discretions.

I hereby revoke any and all general powers of attorney and special powers of attorney that previously have been signed by me. However, the preceding sentence shall not have the effect of revoking any powers of attorney that are directly related to my health care that previously have been signed by me.

My Agent shall have full power and authority to act on my behalf. This power and authority shall authorize my Agent to manage and conduct all of my affairs and to exercise all of my legal rights and powers, including all rights and powers that I may acquire in the future. My Agent's powers shall include, but not be limited to, the power to:

1. Open, maintain or close bank accounts (including, but not limited to, checking accounts, savings accounts, and certificates of deposit), brokerage accounts, retirement plan accounts, and other similar accounts with financial institutions.

   a. Conduct any business with any banking or financial institution with respect to any of my accounts, including, but not limited to, making deposits and withdrawals; negotiating or endorsing any checks or other instruments with respect to any such accounts; and obtaining bank statements, passbooks, drafts, money orders, warrants, and certificates or vouchers payable to me by any person, firm, corporation or political entity.

b. Perform any act necessary to deposit, negotiate, sell, or transfer any note, security, or draft of the United States of America, including U.S. Treasury Securities.

c. Have access to any safe deposit box that I might own, including its contents.

2. Sell, exchange, buy, invest, or reinvest any assets or property owned by me. Such assets or property may include income-producing or non-income-producing assets and property.

3. Take any and all legal steps necessary to collect any amount or debt owed to me, or to settle any claim, whether made against me or asserted on my behalf against any other person or entity.

4. Enter into binding contracts on my behalf.

5. Exercise all stock rights on my behalf as my proxy, including all rights with respect to stocks, bonds, debentures, commodities, options, or other investments.

6. Maintain and/or operate any business that I may own.

7. Employ professional and business assistance as may be appropriate, including attorneys, accountants, and real estate agents.

8. Sell, convey, lease, mortgage, manage, insure, improve, repair, or perform any other act with respect to any of my property (now owned or later acquired), including, but not limited to, real estate and real estate rights (including the right to remove tenants and to recover possession). This includes the right to sell or encumber any homestead that I now own or may own in the future.

9. Prepare, sign, and file documents with any governmental body or agency, including, but not limited to, authorization to:

   a. Prepare, sign and file income and other tax returns with federal, state, local, and other governmental bodies.

   b. Obtain information or documents from any government or its agencies and represent me in all tax matters, including the authority to negotiate, compromise, or settle any matter with such government or agency.

   c. Prepare applications, provide information, and perform any other act reasonably requested by any government or its agencies in connection with governmental benefits (including medical, military, and social security benefits), and to appoint anyone, including my Agent, to act as my "Representative Payee" for the purpose of receiving social security benefits.

10. Make gifts from my assets to members of my family and to such other persons or charitable organizations with whom I have an established pattern of giving (or if it is appropriate to make such gifts for estate planning and/or tax pur-

poses), to file state and federal gift tax returns, and to file a tax election to split gifts with my spouse, if any. No Agent acting under this instrument, except as specifically authorized in this instrument, shall have the power or authority to (a) gift, appoint, assign, or designate any of my assets, interests, or rights, directly or indirectly, to such Agent, such Agent's estate, such Agent's creditors, or the creditors of such Agent's estate; (b) exercise any powers of appointment I may hold in favor of such Agent, such Agent's estate, such Agent's creditors, or the creditors of such Agent's estate; or (c) use any of my assets to discharge any of such Agent's legal obligations, including any obligations of support that such Agent may owe to others, excluding those whom I am legally obligated to support. For the purposes of making gifts to individuals under this provision, I appoint **[name of gift agent]**, of **[address]**, **[city]**, **[state/province]** **[zip/postal code]**, as my "Gift Agent." Provided that they are not the same person, my Agent is authorized to make gifts, as appropriate, to my Gift Agent, and my Gift Agent is authorized to make gifts, as appropriate, to my Agent. Any gifts made to or for the benefit of my Agent or Gift Agent shall be limited to gifts that qualify for the federal gift tax annual exclusion, shall not exceed in value the federal gift tax annual exclusion amount in any one calendar year, and this annual right shall be non-cumulative and shall lapse at the end of each calendar year. If my Agent makes gifts to minors, such gifts may be made directly to the minor; a parent, guardian, or next friend of the minor; or under the Uniform Gifts to Minors Act or the Uniform Transfers to Minors Act.

11. Transfer any of my assets to the trustee of any revocable trust created by me, if such trust is in existence at the time of such transfer.

12. Subject to other provisions of this document, disclaim any interest that might otherwise be transferred or distributed to me from any other person, estate, trust, or other entity, as may be appropriate. However, my Agent may not disclaim assets to which I would be entitled if the result is that the disclaimed assets pass directly or indirectly to my Agent or my Agent's estate. Provided that they are not the same person, my Agent may disclaim assets that pass to my Gift Agent, and my Gift Agent may disclaim assets that pass to my Agent.

This Power of Attorney shall be construed broadly as a General Power of Attorney. The listing of specific powers is not intended to limit or restrict the general powers granted in this Power of Attorney in any manner.

Any power or authority granted to my Agent under this document shall be limited to the extent necessary to prevent this Power of Attorney from causing: (i) my income to be taxable to my Agent, (ii) my assets to be subject to a general power of appointment by my Agent, or (iii) my Agent to have any incidents of ownership with respect to any life insurance policies that I may own on the life of my Agent.

My Agent shall not be liable for any loss that results from a judgment error that was made in good faith. However, my Agent shall be liable for willful misconduct or the failure to act in good faith while acting under the authority of this Power of Attorney. A successor Agent shall not be liable for acts of a prior Agent.

No person who relies in good faith on the authority of my Agent under this instrument shall incur any liability to me, my estate, or my personal representative. I authorize my Agent to indemnify and hold harmless any third party who accepts and acts under this document.

If any part of any provision of this instrument shall be invalid or unenforceable under applicable law, such part shall be ineffective to the extent of such invalidity only, without in any way affecting the remaining parts of such provision or the remaining provisions of this instrument.

My Agent shall be entitled to reasonable compensation for any services provided as my Agent. My Agent shall be entitled to reimbursement of all reasonable expenses incurred as a result of carrying out any provision of this Power of Attorney.

My Agent shall provide an accounting for all funds handled and all acts performed as my Agent, but only if I so request or if such a request is made by any authorized personal representative or fiduciary acting on my behalf.

This Power of Attorney shall become effective immediately, and shall not be affected by my disability or lack of mental competence, except as may be provided otherwise by an applicable state statute. This is a Durable Power of Attorney. This Power of Attorney shall continue effective until my death. This Power of Attorney may be revoked by me at any time by providing written notice to my Agent.

Dated [**month**] [**day**], [**year**], at [**city**], [**state**]

Declarant's name

Witness Signature   Witness Signature

Name   Name

City   City

State   State

STATE OF _____

COUNTY OF _____

In _____, on the
_____ day of _____, 20___, before me, a notary
public in and for the above state and county personally appeared
[**name of person granting power of attorney**], known to me or
proved to be the person whose name is subscribed to the within
instrument and acknowledged to me that he/she executed the
same, and that by his/her signature on the instrument the person
executed the instrument.

_____

NOTARY PUBLIC

My Commission Expires: _____

     (SEAL)

Revocation of Power of Attorney

I, [name of person revoking power of attorney - "principal"], of [city], [state], do hereby revoke the Power of Attorney dated [date power of attorney was authorized], and recorded [place and date power of attorney was recorded], that was granted to [name of person given power of attorney - "attorney-in-fact"], of [city], [state], and withdraw every power and authority conferred therein.

This instrument shall serve as notice to [attorney-in-fact] and to all interested persons that the above Power of Attorney is hereby null and void and of no further force or effect.

IN WITNESS WHEREOF, this instrument is executed under seal on

the _____ day of_____, _____.

Signed, sealed, and delivered in the presence of:

_____

Advance Health Care Directive Form

(CALIFORNIA PROBATE CODE SECTION 4700-4701)

4700. The form provided in Section 4701 may, but need not, be used to create an advance health care directive. The other sections of this division govern the effect of the form or any other writing used to create an advance health care directive. An individual may complete or modify all or any part of the form in Section 4701.

4701. The statutory advance health care directive form is as follows:

ADVANCE HEALTH CARE DIRECTIVE
(California Probate Code Section 4701)

Explanation

You have the right to give instructions about your own health care. You also have the right to name someone else to make health care decisions for you. This form lets you do either, or both, of these things. It also lets you express your wishes regarding donation of organs and the designation of your primary physician. If you use this form, you may complete or modify all or any part of it. You are free to use a different form.

Part One of this form is a power of attorney for health care. Part One lets you name another individual as agent to make health care decisions for you if you become incapable of making your own decisions, or if you want someone else to make those decisions for you now, even though you are still capable. You may also name an alternative agent to act for you if your first choice is not willing, able, or reasonably available to make decisions for you. (Your agent may not be an operator or employee of a community care facility or a residential care facility where you are receiving care, or your supervising health care provider or employee of the health care institution where you are receiving care, unless your agent is related to you or is a coworker.)

Unless the form you sign limits the authority of your agent, your agent may make all health care decisions for you. This form has a place for you to limit the authority of your agent. You need not limit the authority of your agent if you wish to rely on your agent for all health care decisions that may have to be made. If you choose not to limit the authority of your agent, your agent will have the right to:

(a) Consent or refuse consent to any care, treatment, service, or procedure to maintain, diagnose, or otherwise affect a physical or mental condition.

(b) Select or discharge health care providers and institutions.

(c) Approve or disapprove diagnostic tests, surgical procedures, and programs of medication.

(d) Direct the provision, withholding, or withdrawal of artificial nutrition and hydration and all other forms of health care, including cardiopulmonary resuscitation.

(e) Make anatomical gifts, authorize an autopsy, and direct disposition of remains.

Part Two of this form lets you give specific instructions about any aspect of your health care, whether or not you appoint an agent.

Choices are provided for you to express your wishes regarding the provision, withholding, or withdrawal of treatment to keep you alive, as well as the provision of pain relief. Space is also provided for you to add to the choices you have made, or for you to write out any additional wishes. If you are satisfied to allow your agent to determine what is best for you in making end-of-life decisions, you need not fill out Part Two of this form.

Part Three of this form lets you express an intention to donate your bodily organs and tissues following your death.

Part Four of this form lets you designate a physician to have primary responsibility for your health care.

After completing this form, sign and date the form at the end.

The form must be signed by two qualified witnesses or acknowledged before a notary public. Give a copy of the signed and completed form to your physician, any other health care providers you may have, any health care institution at which you are receiving care, and any health care agents you have named. You should talk to the person you have named as agent to make sure that he or she understands your wishes and is willing to take the responsibility.

You have the right to revoke this advance health care directive or replace this form at any time.

Power of Attorney for Health Care

PART ONE

(1.1) DESIGNATION OF AGENT: I designate the following individual as my agent to make health care decisions for me:

_____

(name of individual you choose as agent)

_____

(address) (city) (state) (ZIP Code)

_____

(home phone) (work phone)

OPTIONAL: If I revoke my agent's authority, or if my agent is not willing, able, or reasonably available to make a health care decision for me, I designate as my first alternative agent:

_____

(name of individual you choose as a first alternative agent)

_____

(address) (city) (state) (ZIP Code)

_____

(home phone) (work phone)

OPTIONAL: If I revoke the authority of my agent and first alternative agent, or if neither is willing, able, or reasonably available to make a health care decision for me, I designate as my second alternative agent:

_____

(name of individual you choose as a second alternative agent)

(address) (city) (state) (ZIP Code)

(home phone) (work phone)

(1.2)   AGENT'S AUTHORITY: My agent is authorized to make all health care decisions for me, including decisions to provide, withhold, or withdraw artificial nutrition and hydration, and all other forms of health care to keep me alive, except as I state here:

(Add additional sheets if needed)

(1.3)   WHEN AGENT'S AUTHORITY BECOMES EFFECTIVE: My agent's authority becomes effective when my primary physician determines that I am unable to make my own health care decisions, unless I mark the following box.

If I mark this box [ ], my agent's authority to make health care decisions for me takes effect immediately.

(1.4)   AGENT'S OBLIGATION: My agent shall make health care decisions for me in accordance with this power of attorney for health care, any instructions I give in Part Two of this form, and my other wishes to the extent known to my agent. To the extent my wishes are unknown, my agent shall make health care decisions for me in accordance with what my agent determines to be in my best interest. In determining my best interest, my agent shall consider my personal values to the extent known to my agent.

(1.5) AGENT'S POST-DEATH AUTHORITY: My agent is authorized to make anatomical gifts, authorize an autopsy, and direct disposition of my remains, except as I state here or in Part Three of this form:

_____

_____

(Add additional sheets if needed)

(1.6) NOMINATION OF CONSERVATOR: If a conservator of my person needs to be appointed for me by a court, I nominate the agent designated in this form. If that agent is not willing, able, or reasonably available to act as conservator, I nominate the alternative agents whom I have named, in the order designated.

PART TWO
INSTRUCTIONS FOR HEALTH CARE

If you fill out this part of the form, you may strike any wording you do not want.

(2.1) END-OF-LIFE DECISIONS: I direct that my health care providers and others involved in my care provide, withhold, or withdraw treatment in accordance with the choice I have marked below:

☐ (a) Choice Not To Prolong Life. I do not want my life to be prolonged if:

(1) I have an incurable and irreversible condition that will result in my death within a relatively short time;

(2) I become unconscious and, to a reasonable degree

of medical certainty, I will not regain consciousness; or (3) the likely risks and burdens of treatment would outweigh the expected benefits.

OR

☐ (b)   Choice To Prolong Life. I want my life to be prolonged as long as possible within the limits of generally accepted health care standards.

(2.2)   RELIEF FROM PAIN: Except as I state in the following space, I direct that treatment for alleviation of pain or discomfort be provided at all times, even if it hastens my death:

_____

_____

(Add additional sheets if needed)

(2.3)   OTHER WISHES: (If you do not agree with any of the optional choices above and wish to write your own, or if you wish to add to the instructions you have given above, you may do so here.)

I direct that:

_____

_____

(Add additional sheets if needed)

PART THREE
DONATION OF ORGANS AT DEATH
(OPTIONAL)

(3.1) Upon my death (mark applicable box):

☐ (a) I give any needed organs, tissues, or parts; OR

☐ (b) I give the following organs, tissues, or parts only.

_____

(c) My gift is for the following purposes (strike any of the following you do not want):

(1) Transplant

(2) Therapy

(3) Research

(4) Education

PART FOUR
PRIMARY PHYSICIAN
(OPTIONAL)

(4.1)   I designate the following physician as my primary physician:

_____

(name of physician)

_____

(address) (city) (state) (ZIP Code)

_____

(phone)

OPTIONAL: If the physician I have designated above is not willing, able, or reasonably available to act as my primary physician, I designate the following physician as my primary physician:

_____

(name of physician)

_____

(address) (city) (state) (ZIP Code)

_____

(phone)

PART FIVE

(5.1) EFFECT OF COPY: A copy of this form has the same effect as the original.

(5.2) SIGNATURE: Sign and date the form here:

_____   _____

(date)   *(sign your name)*

_____   _____

(address)   *(print your name)*

_____   _____

(city)   *(state)*

(5.3) STATEMENT OF WITNESSES: I declare under penalty of perjury under the laws of California (1) that the individual who signed or acknowledged this advance health care directive is personally known to me, or that the individual's identity was proved to me by convincing evidence; (2) that the individual signed or acknowledged this advance directive in my presence; (3) that the individual appears to be of sound mind and under no duress, fraud, or undue influence; (4) that I am not a person appointed as agent by this advance directive; and (5) that I am not the individual's health care provider, an employee of the individual's health care provider, the operator of a community care facility, an employee of an operator of a of a community care facility, the operator of a residential care facility for the elderly, or an employee of an operator of a residential care facility for the elderly.

(first witness)	*(second witness)*
(print name)	*(print name)*
(address)	*(address)*
(city, state)	*(city, state)*
(signature of witness)	*(signature of witness)*
(date)	*(date)*

(5.4) ADDITIONAL STATEMENT OF WITNESSES: At least one of the above witnesses must also sign the following declaration:

I further declare under penalty of perjury under the laws of California that I am not related to the individual executing this advance health care directive by blood, marriage, or adoption, and to the best of my knowledge, I am not entitled to any part of the individual's estate upon his or her death under a will now existing or by operation of law.

_____   _____
(signature of witness)   *(signature of witness)*

PART SIX
SPECIAL WITNESS REQUIREMENT

(6.1) The following statement is required only if you are a patient in a skilled nursing facility — a health care facility that provides the following basic services: skilled nursing care and supportive care to patients whose primary need is for availability of skilled nursing care on an extended basis. The patient advocate or ombudsman must sign the following statement:

STATEMENT OF PATIENT ADVOCATE OR OMBUDSMAN

I declare under penalty of perjury under the laws of California that I am a patient advocate or ombudsman as designated by the State Department of Aging, and that I am serving as a witness as required by Section 4675 of the Probate Code.

_____   _____
(date)   *(sign your name)*

_____   _____
(address)   *(print your name)*

_____   _____
(city)   *(state)*

Pennsylvania Out-of-Hospital Do-Not-Resuscitate Order

"Patient's full legal name: _____

I, the undersigned, state that I am the attending physician of the patient named above. The above-named patient has requested this order, and I have made the determination that this patient is in a terminal condition and eligible for an order.

I direct any and all emergency medical services personnel, commencing on the effective date of this order, to withhold cardiopulmonary resuscitation (cardiac compression, invasive airway techniques, artificial ventilation, defibrillation, and other related procedures) from the patient in the event of the patient's respiratory or cardiac arrest. I further direct such personnel to provide to the patient other medical interventions, such as intravenous fluids, oxygen, or other therapies necessary to provide comfort or to alleviate pain, unless directed otherwise by the patient or the emergency medical services provider's authorized medical command physician.

_____
Signature of attending physician

_____
Printed name of attending physician

_____
Date

_____
Attending physician's emergency telephone number

I, the undersigned, hereby direct that, in the event of my cardiac and/or respiratory arrest, efforts at cardiopulmonary resuscitation not be initiated. I understand that I may revoke these directions at any time by giving verbal instructions to the emergency medical services providers, by physical cancellation or destruction of this form or my bracelet or necklace, or by simply not displaying this form or the bracelet or necklace for my EMS caregivers.

_____

Signature of patient (if capable of making informed decisions)

I, the undersigned, hereby certify that I am authorized to execute this order on the patient's behalf by virtue of having been designated as the patient's surrogate, and/or by virtue of my relationship to the patient (specify relationship: _____).
I hereby direct that, in the event of the patient's cardiac and/or respiratory arrest, efforts at cardiopulmonary resuscitation not be initiated."

_____

Signature of surrogate (if patient is capable of making informed decisions)

The statute also provides that this order may be revoked by the patient or surrogate.

Statutory Living Will Form in North Carolina

ADVANCE DIRECTIVE FOR A NATURAL DEATH ("LIVING WILL")

NOTE: YOU SHOULD USE THIS DOCUMENT TO GIVE YOUR HEALTH CARE PROVIDERS INSTRUCTIONS TO WITHHOLD OR WITHDRAW LIFE-PROLONGING MEASURES IN CERTAIN SITUATIONS. THERE IS NO LEGAL REQUIREMENT THAT ANYONE EXECUTE A LIVING WILL.

GENERAL INSTRUCTIONS: You can use this Advance Directive ("Living Will") form to give instructions for the future if you want your health care providers to withhold or withdraw life-prolonging measures in certain situations. You should talk to your doctor about what these terms mean. The Living Will states what choices you would have made for yourself if you were able to communicate. Talk to your family members, friends, and others you trust about your choices. Also, it is a good idea to talk with professionals, such as your doctors, clergypersons, and lawyers before you complete and sign this Living Will.

You do not have to use this form to give those instructions, but if you create your own Advance Directive, you need to be very careful to ensure that it is consistent with North Carolina law.

This Living Will form is intended to be valid in any jurisdiction in which it is presented, but places outside North Carolina may impose requirements that this form does not meet.

If you want to use this form, you must complete it, sign it, and have your signature witnessed by two qualified witnesses and proved by a *notary public. Follow the instructions about which choices you can ini-tial very carefully. Do not sign this form until two witnesses and a notary public are present to watch you sign it. You should then con-sider giving a copy to your primary physician and/or a trusted relative, and should consider filing it with the Advanced Health Care Directive Registry maintained by the North Carolina Secretary of State: **www. nclifelinks.org/ahcdr.**

My Desire for a Natural Death

I, _____, being of sound mind, desire that, as specified below, my life not be prolonged by life-prolonging measures:

1. When My Directives Apply

My directions about prolonging my life shall apply **IF** my attend-ing physician determines that I lack capacity to make or commu-nicate health care decisions and:

NOTE: YOU MAY INITIAL ANY AND ALL OF THESE CHOICES.

_____ I have an incurable or irreversible condition that will
(Initial)   result in my death within a relatively short period of time.

_____ I become unconscious and my health care providers
(Initial)   determine that, to a high degree of medical certainty, I will never regain my consciousness.

_____ I suffer from advanced dementia or any other condi-
(Initial)   tion that results in the substantial loss of my cogni-tive ability, and my health care providers determine

that, to a high degree of medical certainty, this loss is not reversible.

2. These Are My Directives About Prolonging My Life:

In those situations I have initialed in Section One, I direct that my health care providers:

NOTE: INITIAL ONLY IN ONE PLACE.

_____ may withhold or withdraw life-prolonging measures.
(Initial)

_____ shall withhold or withdraw life-prolonging measures.
(Initial)

3. Exceptions — "Artificial Nutrition or Hydration"

NOTE: INITIAL ONLY IF YOU WANT TO MAKE EXCEPTIONS TO YOUR INSTRUCTIONS IN PARAGRAPH TWO.

EVEN THOUGH I do not want my life prolonged in those situations I have initialed in Section One:

_____ I *DO* want to receive BOTH artificial hydration *and*
(Initial)   artificial nutrition (for example, through tubes) in those situations.

NOTE: DO NOT INITIAL THIS BLOCK IF ONE OF THE BLOCKS BELOW IS INITIALED.

_____ I *DO* want to receive ONLY artificial hydration (for ex-
(Initial)   ample, through tubes) in those situations.

NOTE: DO NOT INITIAL THE BLOCK ABOVE OR BELOW IF THIS BLOCK IS INITIALED.

_____ I *DO* want to receive ONLY artificial nutrition (for ex-
(Initial)   ample, through tubes) in those situations.

NOTE: DO NOT INITIAL EITHER OF THE TWO BLOCKS ABOVE IF THIS BLOCK IS INITIALED.

4. I Wish To Be Made as Comfortable as Possible

I direct that my health care providers take reasonable steps to keep me as clean, comfortable, and free of pain as possible so that my dignity is maintained, even though this care may hasten my death.

5. I Understand My Advance Directive

I am aware and understand that this document directs certain life-prolonging measures to be withheld or discontinued in accordance with my advance instructions.

6. If I Have an Available Health Care Agent

If I have appointed a health care agent by executing a health care power of attorney or similar instrument, and that health care agent is acting and available and gives instructions that differ from this Advance Directive, I direct that:

_____ Follow Advance Directive: This Advance Directive will override instructions my health care agent gives about prolonging my life.

_____ Follow Health Care Agent: My health care agent has
(Initial) authority to override this Advance Directive.

NOTE: DO NOT INITIAL BOTH BLOCKS. IF YOU DO NOT INITIAL EITHER BOX, THEN YOUR HEALTH CARE PROVIDERS WILL FOLLOW THIS ADVANCE DIRECTIVE AND IGNORE THE INSTRUCTIONS OF YOUR HEALTH CARE AGENT ABOUT PROLONGING YOUR LIFE.

7. My Health Care Providers May Rely On This Directive

My health care providers shall not be liable to me or to my family, my estate, my heirs, or my personal representative for following the instructions I give in this instrument. Following my directions shall not be considered suicide, or the cause of my death, or malpractice, or unprofessional conduct. If I have revoked this instrument, but my health care providers do not know that I have done so and follow the instructions in this instrument in good faith, they shall be entitled to the same protections to which they would have been entitled if the instrument had not been revoked.

8. I Want This Directive To Be Effective Anywhere

I intend that this Advance Directive be followed by any health care provider in any place.

9. I Have the Right to Revoke This Advance Directive

I understand that at any time I may revoke this Advance Directive in a writing I sign, or by communicating in any clear and consistent manner my intent to revoke it to my attending physician. I understand that if I revoke this instrument, I should try to destroy all copies of it.

This, the _____ day of _____, _____.

_____
Print Name

I hereby state that the declarant, _____, being of sound mind, signed (or directed another to sign on declarant's behalf) the foregoing Advance Directive for a Natural Death in my presence, and that I am not related to the declarant by blood or marriage, and I would not be entitled to any portion of the estate of the declarant under any existing will or codicil of the declarant or as an heir under the Intestate Succession Act, if the declarant died on this date without a will. I also state that I am not the declarant's attending physician or a licensed health care provider who is (1) an employee of the declarant's attending physician, (2) nor an employee of the health facility in which the declarant is a patient, or (3) an employee of a nursing home or any adult care home where the declarant resides. I further state that I do not have any claim against the declarant or the estate of the declarant.

_____
Date

_____
Witness

_____
Date

_____
Witness

_____COUNTY, _____STATE

Sworn to (or affirmed) and subscribed before me this day by ___

_____

_____

_____
(type/print name of declarant)

_____
(type/print name of witness)

_____
(type/print name of witness)

Date: _____

_____   _____
(Official Seal)   *Signature of Notary Public*

_____, Notary Public
Printed or typed name

My commission expires: _____

GLOSSARY OF TERMS

The many different terms used in estate planning are often confusing. Here are some of which you need to take note. These are simple, brief definitions of some terms you will find in this book. Make sure you consider that there might be differences in how they are used.

401(k). A retirement account provided by employers. Employees pay no taxes on money placed in a 401(k) until they take it out at retirement. Employers may add matching funds to the account.

AB Trust. An AB Trust is one that establishes two trusts, one for each spouse. The surviving spouse can then use the property in the other's trust, but avoids double taxation on the property from when one spouse dies to when the second spouse dies.

Abatement. This is the process of pulling back specific gifts under a will when it becomes necessary to create a fund to meet expenses or to pay taxes, or in other specific situations.

Abstract of Trust. This tool allows you to say that your trust exists and that it will be used. It is a "short list" of what is included in that trust, rather than spelling it all out.

Ademption. In ademption statutes, laws are in place which protect heirs that do not or cannot receive what you leave to them in your will. If you leave property in your will and estate to someone, and that property is no longer part of your estate, this statute defines what should happen.

Agent. The person named by a power of attorney to handle health care or legal and financial matters for someone else.

Attorney-in-Fact. The person named by a power of attorney to handle health care or legal and financial matters for someone else.

Basis. The tax basis is the value that is assigned to the property from which taxable gain or loss on a sale is determined. This means that when property is purchased, its basis tends to be the cost.

Beneficiary. A beneficiary is an individual or a group that benefits from the gifts made under a legal document, which can include wills, trusts, pay on death accounts, retirement plans, and insurance products. This is the person that gets something from these documents.

Child's Trust. A trust that is created solely for the use of one child who is a minor.

Community Property. Property that is shared between you and your spouse in a community living state. This property belongs equally to both parties, as it was obtained during the marriage.

Comprehensive Health-Care Directive. A document that

combines a health care power of attorney with a living will.

Conservatee or Ward. The incapacitated person for whom a conservatorship or guardianship has been established.

Conservator/Guardian. Someone appointed by the court to act for an incapacitated or incompetent person, making either health-care or financial decisions. The terms have different meanings in different states.

Creditor. A company or an organization that is owed money; this is the company that lent you money that you need to repay.

Custodian. Under the Uniform Transfers to Minor Act, this is the person named by you to care for the property that is left to a minor child.

Death Taxes. Death taxes, probate taxes, or estate taxes are taxes that are assessed on the property of a person that has died.

Do-Not-Resuscitate Order (DNR). A directive forbidding the use of CPR if someone's heart stops.

Durable Power of Attorney. The power of attorney that remains effective even when the principal (person that created it) becomes incapacitated. This person is authorized to act in the other's place and is called an attorney-in-fact.

Estate. All the property that you own when you die is your estate. There are various ways of determining the value of your estate, as defined in this book, including your probate estate and taxable estate.

Estate Planning. Planning for what will happen to your estate when you die while you are still alive. It helps you move your estate from your property to that of your heirs in the best manner possible.

Estate Taxes. These are taxes that are applied to your property when you die. There are various tax situations that you could be in; for example, the federal estate tax is levied when a person reaches the estate tax threshold for the year in which they die.

Estate Tax Threshold. The dollar amount, as defined by the federal government, for the year in which you die, at which point taxes are levied on your estate.

Executor. The individual that will manage your estate, move through probate, and collect all your assets. He or she will distribute them to your heirs as you define in your will.

Fiduciary Responsibility. The obligation of trustees and agents to use their authority for the good of the principal and not to enrich themselves.

Final Beneficiaries. Those people that will receive property from your estate.

Fixed-Income Annuities. Issued by insurance companies, these investments pay back a sum every month after they are purchased.

Generation Skipping Trust. This is a trust that is set up to avoid double taxation. The principal leaves the trust for the grandchild rather than for his or her children. This helps avoid taxation from the principal to the child, and then again from the taxation when the child passes it to the grandchild.

Gifts. Property that is given to another person or organization. This can be done throughout life or through trusts, wills, and a living trust after death.

Gift Taxes. Taxes that are levied on any gifts when the gifts are given (usually before death).

Grantor. A grantor is a person that establishes a trust.

Guardian. Someone who has full authority over the health or financial decisions of another individual whom the courts have decided cannot take care of themselves.

Health Care Directive. This document will define the wishes of the document writer in regard to health care when they cannot communicate those wishes themselves. It names a person that will make decisions for them at this time.

Health Care Power of Attorney. A document signed by a person giving someone else the authority to make medical decisions when he or she is incapacitated.

Heirs. Those that will inherit property, by law, at the time of death of those to whom they are related. Heirs will receive property that is not left specifically through a will or trust to someone else.

Holographic Will. Last will and testament completely written in the decedent's own handwriting, signed and dated, but not required to be witnessed; legal only in those states which recognize such a will form.

Inheritance Taxes. Taxes that are imposed on property that is received by heirs at the time of death.

Insurance. A product that is purchased that provides protection from a variety of situations in the event that they happen. Life insurance, for example, provides coverage in a monetary benefit if the insured person dies while the policy is in effect.

International Will. Form of a will specified by Illinois statute for wills executed outside the United States and offered for probate in Illinois.

Irrevocable Trust. A trust that can no longer be changed.

Joint Tenancy. When two or more people own property, the other will become the owner of the entire property when one dies.

Life Beneficiary. This inclusion in an AB Trust allows for the other spouse to take use of the property in Trust A for his or her own needs when the other spouse dies. It does not provide ownership of this property to the spouse, though, which is the key factor in avoiding estate taxes.

Life Insurance Trust. This trust is one that owns a life insurance policy. It helps reduce the size of the original owner's taxable estate.

Living Trust. A living trust is set up while the person is still alive, which allows them to control what is in the trust until they die. It helps minimize the value of property that goes through probate. Grantors are able to specify that the property in the trust will pass right to the beneficiaries at the time of death, avoiding probate.

Marital Deduction. In accordance with tax law, a marital deduction allows all property that is passed from one spouse to the other spouse at the time of death to be free from taxes.

Pay on Death. Variety of methods that are used for the payment of funds at the time of death. It defines who will acquire all that remains in the account when the holder of the account dies.

Power of Attorney. The power of attorney provides legal documentation that the individual is giving authorization for someone other than themselves to act for them.

Probate. Probate is a process that includes several steps. Probate authenticates the will of the deceased, appoints the executor or administrator of your will, pays debts and taxes that are due on the estate, identifies the heirs of the estate, and distributes the property in the will to those that are designated in the will.

QTIP Trust. A Qualified Terminable Interest Property Trust is a trust that does not reduce or stop estate taxes, but it does postpone them. It can be used when an individual estate exceeds the estate tax threshold to postpone the payment of taxes on the estate.

Real Property. Real property is all land and all buildings attached to it, as well as all improvements made to it. It is real estate. Anything that is not real property is considered to be personal property.

Residual Beneficiary. A person who will receive property that is left in a will or trust that is not given to others in that document. It can also mean a person that receives property from a trust when the life beneficiary dies.

Right of Survivorship. When two people own property, this is the right that the joint tenant has in claiming the other's share of the property at the time of death.

Spoliated. Refers to a will that has been ruined in some way that makes it impossible to read, validate, or determine the wishes of the testator.

Successor Trustee. A successor trustee is a person that the creator of the trust places in charge when he or she dies, if he or she is the trustee of the living trust.

Taxable Estate. The value of the estate that is able to be taxed, as it goes over the estate tax threshold or the allowable amount of no taxing.

Tenancy by the Entirety. This form of tenancy is one that is a form of marital property ownership. It provides joint ownership of property to both spouses.

Trust. A legal document and situation in which property is held for the benefit of others. The grantor or trustor places property into the trust that is managed by the trustee until it passes to the beneficiary.

Trustee. The trustee of a trust is the person that will manage the trust for the beneficiary until they can take claim to the property in it.

Trustor. The creator of a trust.

Uniform Transfers to Minors Act. This law provides for the method that property is transferred to minors in the event of a death.

Will. A will is a legal document that defines what the deceased person's wishes are in regard to his or her property. It provides for what his or her intentions are for where property should go after he or she dies.

BIBLIOGRAPHY

Gross, Howard I., and Richards, Pierre E., *The Trustee's Guide: An Essential Handbook for Trustees, Beneficiaries, and Advisors*, LawFirst Publishing, 2003.

Guardian Life Insurance Company of America, **www.guardian-life.com**.

Internal Revenue Service, **www.IRS.gov**.

Metlife: Life Insurance and Other Financial Services, **www.metlife.com**.

NOLO: Legal Solutions for You, Your Family & Your Business, **www.nolo.com**.

Plotnick, Charles K., L.L.B., and Leimberg, Stephan R., J.D., *How to Settle an Estate: A Manual for Executors and Trustees*, Plume, 1998.

Schooley, Tim, "The third generation isn't always a charm," Pittsburgh Business Times, Sept. 17, 2004, **http://pittsburgh.bizjournals.com/pittsburgh/stories/2004/09/20/focus3.html**.

Shenkman, Martin M, *The Complete Book of Trusts*, John Wiley & Sons Inc, 2002.

The University of Texas at Austin, "Grief and Loss," **www.utexas.edu**.

Wilson, Douglas D., CFP, CTFA, *Executor & Trustee Survival Guide*, Fiduciary Publishing, 2001.

AUTHOR BIOGRAPHY

Gerald Shaw served as a personal representative for his family's estate. He is a writer and editor for a book publishing company. He has written on politics, government, financial issues, health, and entertainment for such publications as *Florida Today*, *Daytona Beach News-Journal*, *National Enquirer*, *Globe*, and *Today in PT* magazine. He lives in Edgewater, Florida with his beagle, Yogi.

INDEX